W9-DHT-395

PORTRAIT OF YAHWEH AS A YOUNG GOD

Greta Wels-Schon

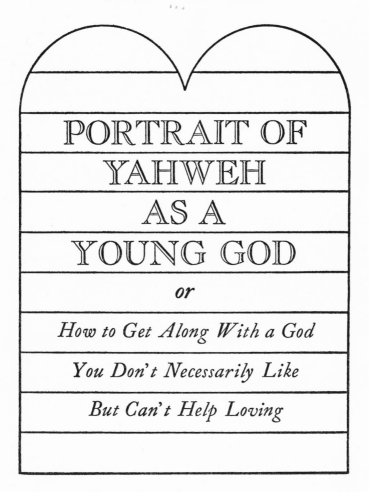

PORTRAIT OF
YAHWEH
AS A
YOUNG GOD

or

How to Get Along With a God

You Don't Necessarily Like

But Can't Help Loving

HOLT, RINEHART *and* WINSTON

NEW YORK   CHICAGO   SAN FRANCISCO

Published simultaneously in Canada by Holt, Rinehart
and Winston of Canada, Ltd.

Library of Congress Catalog Card Number: 68-14929

First Edition

Designed by Bert Waggott
8697252
Printed in the United States of America

To all those

to whom God has ceased to make sense

Contents

Introduction

It STARTED with the Pillars of Hercules. These pillars are the emblem of Spain and one finds them everywhere—as trademarks, on letterheads, and on almost all of the coins—and I wondered what the Spaniards could tell me about them. The first one I asked came up with a rapid and wondrous synopsis: "Hercules," he said, "was a Roman of stupendous strength. When he got hold of the two pillars, he brought the whole house down." Although this piece of information impressed me, I decided that I had better go into the matter on my own.

To get firsthand information about the Pillars of Hercules I had to read the Old Testament, which I had not done for ages. When I settled down to it, I found myself before I knew it involved with God again, whom I had left long ago. The final and totally unexpected result of this adventure was a wholehearted Apology of Yahweh, whom I came to see now as I had seen him never before.

God is no more the God he was. How could it be otherwise if he is the Living God, for life is ceaseless change. Unfortunately this Living God—whose images we are and who is so much of this world—has been transported beyond our reach by theology, which exalted him completely out of this world, out of history and out of life.

Returning to the Old Testament, I found emerging from it

the portrait of Yahweh as a young God, as alive and as close to humanity as no other god. This God meant to make history and he made it; in the Old Testament he has left us his autobiography, ghostwritten by Moses and the Prophets. And with this God I made my peace.

It was only after I had finished my portrait of Yahweh that I was sent Jung's *Answer to Job*. Jung had his encounter with the Old Testament God at about the same age I had mine, but we were separated by one generation, a decisive generation. "He is everything in its totality," Jung rightly remarks about God, "therefore, among other things, he is total justice, and also its total opposite." But when it comes to this "total opposite," Jung is unforgiving. Instead of coming to grips with this God in his totality, with all the horse sense and humor it needs, he starts in earnest a purely gnostic argument, with pleroma and aeons and all the other gnostic trappings. Gnosis had been one of the many highhanded theological attempts, undertaken at the beginning of our era by those who could not square the new God of Greek philosophy with the banausic God of the Jews, who had *made* us not only in his image but *with his own hands*.

Beginning in the fourth century B.C., the Greeks arrived finally by philosophical speculations at an abstract idea of a perfect and immutable God—one of the more undigestible theories they have left us. Yahweh, on the other hand, was neither a philosophical theory nor immutable. He had lived and raged and suffered throughout the Old Testament and had undergone changes, as everything living does. Why, then, are we so shocked when we discover that he had been rather imperfect at times? How could he, the living God who had made us in his image, be perfect when we, his images, are not?

Because we have been conditioned by theology to a very vague abstraction of a God who is not of this world. Gnosis and Christian theology left the embarrassing Yahweh where they had found him—in the Old Testament—and began reshaping God and the world with heavy borrowings from Greek philosophy. Western Christianity solved the paradox of the God who had made Man in his own image with the beloved tale of the Fall of

Man. In Greece, Hesiod had started this hare, which shows that Ionians and Jews had been poaching in a common hunting ground. Plato gave the Fall of Man a great deal of thought, which resulted, with a peculiar sort of logic, in his pessimistic upside-down theory of devolution. There was no such thing as evolution for him. Seeing nothing but degeneration in this world, he turned his back on it and opened a new vista: the Other World, a world of perfection.

The Christians made very heavy weather of the Fall, which became a cornerstone of Western theology. Glorying in the glory of their new and perfectly perfect God, they never tired of rubbing the nose of Man in "his inheritance of misery after the Fall." What could there be in store for these fallen wretches but the end of the world! Yet it never came. When Aristotle was rediscovered, Thomas Aquinas made a grandiose attempt to introduce reason into a totally irrational theology. His declaration that God was pure reason aroused the protest of Duns Scotus: God is not pure reason, he stated; God is pure will. He could be whatever he willed to be; therefore he could also be irrational if he so willed. This made better sense than the claim for reason, but Greek theories again swamped Christian thinking, as they had done at its very beginning. During twenty centuries, a theological jungle of impenetrable density had grown around what had been God, who consequently got so completely lost from sight that we felt entitled to question his existence.

As I burrowed deep into the Old Testament in search of the authentic pillars of Hercules, the unexpected encounter with Yahweh gave me a wholesome shake-up. After I had moved in circles who talked about the Ultimate Reality or whatever the latest God-substitute is, an initial shock was inevitable when I found myself confronted with this almost-forgotten God, who had made the world and us and who constantly had tantrums because his creation did not work the way he had wanted it to. I was bewildered; I even was peeved—which angered me—but not for long. Trying to get things straight, I found that there was no dilemma to begin with, because the Ultimate Reality is a metaphysical principle, which did not interest me, while Yahweh was a historical fact, which aroused my curiosity. So I began to follow his history—maliciously at first, then with growing fascination, until all of a sudden understanding dawned. And coming to know him, I found at last a most comforting *modus vivendi* with him—still teasing him, but with great fondness now.

This happy end was not reached by a flying leap. It took considerable meanderings and apropos. Since, during my long life, I had learned slowly that systematic thinking, deductive, inductive or otherwise, had been a) highly overrated and b) hardly ever practiced, that Aristotelian logic had been a strait jacket to thinking, and that the syllogism had gone the way of all flesh, I decided to go by common sense and to let the sense of humor loose, which I found always helpful when clouds of seriousness threatened to dim the view. This latter tendency seemed to be in the air, as I saw to my delight in a review of Father Hugo Rahner's latest book *Man at Play, Or Did You Ever Practice Eutrapelia?* Father Rahner stresses the need of *eutrapelia*, playfulness and wit, as a "healing necessity, trapped as we are on the helplessly wrong road of idiotic earnestness." What a joy, hearing this from a clergyman's mouth! It had been just this—my proclivity for playful and loose thinking—that led me to discover in Yahweh the "Friend behind phenomena," as he was named by Gilbert Murray.

I left the event where it took place, that is where Yahweh had his historical epiphany—between the Pillars of Hercules. As for these pillars, instead of repeating what can be found in Frazer's *Golden Bough* and in the endless flood of Freemason literature, I looked for bits of evidence in numismatics, archaeology, and ancient history, especially the Old Testament, the Greek historians and—by a lucky strike—the Abbé Pluche.

PORTRAIT OF YAHWEH AS A YOUNG GOD

The Pillars of Hercules I

OF COURSE, the Greeks had a name for them. It was a misnomer, but, as usual, it only added to their vast prestige.

These pillars must have galled the Greeks. Wherever they turned, they always encountered them, which meant that the Phoenicians had been there before them. Something had to be done, and so they called them Pillars of Hercules, although the pillars existed before Hercules ever did. It was their way of out-smarting the Phoenicians, who, as sailors and merchants, were smarter than the Greeks. These ancient mariners had crossed the Mediterranean, reached the Atlantic, and founded Gades, where, as Diodorus Siculus tells us, "they built a stately temple to Hercules and instituted splendid sacrifices to be offered to him after the rites and customs *of the Phoenicians*" (here and elsewhere, all italics mine) .

Now who is this Hercules really? Herodotus' answer shows that by his time the muddle was already deep: "Wishing to get the best information I could on these matters, I made a voyage to Tyre in Phoenicia, hearing there was a temple of Hercules at that place" (2:44) . He inspects the place and the pillars, one of gold and one of glass, and interviews the priests. Seeing another temple dedicated to the Thasian Hercules, he decides he must find out about this one too: "So I went on to Thasos where I found a temple of Hercules, built by the Phoenicians who colonized the island when they sailed in search of Europa. Even this was five generations earlier than the time when Hercules, son of Amphitryon, was born in Greece. These researches show plainly that there is an ancient god Hercules."

This is quite clear, but four hundred years later Diodorus had to start all over again. He wrestles for many pages with several Herculeses and, exhausted in the end, summarizes briefly: "The last Hercules was the son of Zeus by Alcmena, born a little after the Trojan War: he travelled through many parts of the world to execute the commands of Eurystheus, and succeeded in all his enterprises: he erected a pillar in Europe. Because his name was the same and his actions were similar to those of the ancient Herculeses, after their deaths posterity ascribed the things they had done solely to him, *as if there never had been any but one Hercules in the world.*"

I share Diodorus' indignation, and fully agree with him when in Book 5 he once again grumbles about "the ignorance of the vulgar" who cannot tell one Hercules from another. I must admit that, in my vulgar ignorance, I have a pretty hard time sorting them out, and the whole business reminds me more and more of Mark Twain's solution to the Shakespeare question: the Pillars of Hercules were not erected by Hercules, but by another god of the same name.

Strabo starts a good pillar-argument. Neither Calpe and Ceuta, flanking the Straits of Gibraltar, nor the little islands called Pillars of Hercules will do, he says, for the very simple reason that "neither the little islands, nor yet the mountains, bear much resemblance to pillars, and we should seek for pillars strictly so called." For, he writes, it is an ancient usage to set up pillars, altars or towers as boundary marks, as, for instance, Alexander did on his march to India. Later, after these landmarks have fallen to ruin and are gone, the name still clings to the place where they were erected.

Towards the end of his argument, Strabo reaches "the pillars of brass in the temple of Hercules at Gades, on which is inscribed the cost of erecting that edifice, and the fact that the sailors coming there on completion of their voyages and sacrificing to Hercules rendered the place so famous that it came to be

regarded as the termination of the land and sea." But with
Alexander still in his mind, he is carried away in the wrong direction; befogged by the name Hercules and the glory that is
Greece, he concludes: "It seems most likely that the name was
originally conferred, not by merchants, *but by generals,* its
celebrity afterwards becoming universal, as was the case with the
Indian pillars. Besides, the inscription recorded refutes that
idea, since it contains no religious dedication but a mere list of
the expenses; whereas *the pillars of Hercules should have been a
record of the hero's wonderful deeds,* not of Phoenician expen-
diture" (3.5.5–6).

Three cheers for Strabo! In telling us what the pillars should
have been, but were not, he reveals their origin: they were not
erected by Greek generals, but by Phoenician merchants who, as
good businessmen, marked down the sum they had spent in
honor of their god. Wherever they had trading posts they
erected an altar and two pillars, a high place, and sacrificed to
their god Melkarth, the city-god of Tyre, Phoenicia's capital at
the time of the Prophets. We know him well from the Bible,
and without him the Old Testament would be a mere short
story. We know him best as Baal.

The Greeks simply called him Hercules, and, in doing so, they
unwittingly confused the picture for all time. Their Hercules
myth could have been created by their Ministry of Propaganda,
to make their colonial claims legitimate. Pillars of Hercules were
reported by ancient authors from quite a number of places, and
thus Hercules had to become a far-flung hero, making the whole
known world potentially Greek. It was obviously a difficult task
for mythographers, who produced half a dozen Herculeses and
finally packed every stray myth and ritual into the Hercules
cycle, until it became a huge, shapeless and rather transparent
bag of arbitrary adaptation and aetiological invention. It was
the fabrication of several generations, dear to Graecomaniacs.
Herodotus, not being one, shrugged: "The Greeks tell many
tales without due investigation." Pliny was more determined:
"But the traditions respecting Hercules I conceive to be fabulous in the highest degree."

The ancient writers knew it. But today, roughly two thousand years later, many of us, indoctrinated by the wrong classical scholars, still accredit the Greeks with the pillars, although they have nothing to do with the misogynous Greek hero who fought indefatigably for men's rights, subduing lions, bulls, boars, and women.

The Pillars of Hercules are most significant in the furnishings of the Baal cult, flourishing in the Levant. They were not structural columns but the two pillars flanking the altars and, later, the entrance to the temples. None of the temples has survived. The pillars have, in their way, as we shall see. From Megalithic times, through the Bronze and Iron Ages, down to the beginning of our era, the whole Near East had a dense growth of sacred pillars, obelisks, holy cones, stones, poles, and baetyls. They represented the abode of gods and goddesses; they also marked the sites of memorable events, and they were altogether numinous. The Bible shows us Jacob, among others, setting up stones on suitable occasions and anointing them. According to tradition he did this about 1700 B.C., and it was a praiseworthy act.

But hardly a thousand years later, the Old Testament rings with the lamentations of the Prophets about the "stocks and stones" of the immensely popular Baal and Asherah worship around them. And not only the Canaanites, Phoenicians, and Syrians were ardent followers of Baal, but also the Israelites—on and off—as testified by the Prophets. They worshiped the Canaanite Baal, or their own Yahweh as Baal, in the shape of a bullock, the "golden calf" they had already danced around while Moses was on Sinai. But more often it was the pillars that outraged the Prophets.

The purely generic "stocks and stones" of the King James Bible are to the point, while "images" and "groves" are nearly always misleading. "Their groves by the green trees upon the high hills" in Jeremiah (17:2) does not make any sense, and the Glossary of Antiquities attached to the Sunday School Teacher's Edition of the Holy Bible says: "Grove is often a mistranslation for the *wooden image* of Ashtaroth, or Astarte, the moon, or chief female goddess of Baalism." Unfortunately this correction too is misleading, for the object in question is aniconic and therefore not a "wooden image" but the "stock," the wooden pillar, habitual abode of Asherah. This stock was also called an asherah, to add to the confusion, and was always placed *in a grove of trees.*

The incessant misuse of "image" is just as disconcerting in the Bible as it is in our contemporary language: "New image for wool needed," or "Banana Republics in need of new image."

Take this passage from II Chronicles 34:4. "And they brake down the altars of Baalim in his presence, and the images that were on high above them he cut down, and the groves and the carved images and the molten images he brake in pieces. . . ." Now, what on earth are the first "images"? In the margin the Bible says "sun-images," which does not help much. But Luther's translation *"Sonnensäulen,"* which means sun-pillars, hits the nail! It is again an aniconic object and not an image. Luther's biblical glossary says: "Sun-pillars, erected at the altars of Baal and dedicated to him as sun-god." And now the ritual furnishing that we met in the passage above becomes clear: the horned altars, the sun-pillars of Baal, the moon-pillar of Asherah, carved wooden statues, and molten bronze statues. Here we have a fully equipped high place.

High places are sanctuaries, open-air cult precincts placed on hilltops, and certainly the most sanitary sanctuaries imaginable, considering the perpetual sacrificial slaughter which ancient gods, including Yahweh, demanded. Before they had the Temple, Israel had high places like anybody else at that time. And after the Temple, they got the pillars, like everybody else. When they arrived at Sinai, the first thing Moses did was erect pillars (Exod. 24:4). And it is always other people's pillars or high places which are abominable. That seems to be a universal religious law. The Israelites' "great high place" was at Gibeon, where they kept the Ark of the Covenant and the horned altar, made at Yahweh's special order (Exod. 30). The whole Near East, including Crete and Mycenae, had horned altars.

If we want to know more about the Pillars of Hercules, we must have a look at the Temple in Jerusalem; we can follow its building in bewildering detail in the books of Kings and Chronicles. Solomon, in need of raw materials and skilled labor, makes a deal with Hiram, King of Tyre, who in the end felt cheated and said so (I Kings 9:12–13). However, the Phoenicians came and built the Temple, and being Phoenicians, they must have made it a gorgeous and gaudy affair, with—needless to say—two pillars flanking the entrance "eighteen cubits high apiece: and a line of twelve cubits did encompass either of them" (I Kings 7:15).

Recent excavations near Tel Aviv have shown that the entrance flanked by two pillars was evidently already the standard temple in the third millennium B.C. An article by Jean Perrot in the *Illustrated London News* (Dec. 16, 1960) shows a marvelous find of ossuaries, so-called house urns. "Of particular interest," writes Mr. Perrot, "is the façade of an ossuary in the first group, where the door is flanked by two poles which project above the façade and terminate as capitals; more decorative than functional, these poles could have a symbolic significance. They lead one to remember the masts and columns flanking the entrances of later Phoenician and Assyrian temples." Solomon had them in front of his temple. And, being a wise man who wanted to live in peace, he also had a few precincts built for his foreign wives, where they could worship in their own way. How these looked we are not told, but now we know: there was no high place and no temple without the pillars, pillarlike towers, or obelisks. They flanked the temples of Mesopotamia, the temple of Aphrodite in Paphos on Cyprus, and the temples of Baal, also called Melkarth, the Phoenician Hercules of Tyre.

When the Phoenicians landed in Spain, the America of antiquity, they put their pillars on Spanish soil. And when roughly twenty-five hundred years later the Spaniards landed in America, they put the pillars on their colonial coins. These pillars, "encompassed by a line" in S-form, are the sign of the dollar—$. A mighty symbol they are, and of a longevity and secular power that surpasses the imagination of any prophet. And again an angry old man, this time a Russian, cursed them and prophesied the downfall of those who worship them and what they stand for. And I wonder.

Apropos One

BEFORE WE PURSUE these pillars any further, we should have a look at the ethnic make-up of the Near Eastern locale. Being the crossroad of three continents, the Levant has always been an unusual racial melting pot. Professor W. F. Albright tells us that "to the astonishment of the scientific world," in Palestine even Homo neanderthalensis and Homo sapiens had been interbreeding, as skeletal finds have proved. This astonishing event took place in one of those almost meaninglessly remote geological phases, called Riss-Würm. "It would appear that Homo sapiens came from the southeast into Europe, driving Neanderthaloid man before him and interbreeding with the conquered foe at the same time," writes Albright (*The Archaeology of Palestine*, p. 55). But when a speaker at the Congress of Physical Anthropologists, held in Copenhagen just before World War II, referred to this fact and said with a twinkle that "Homo sapiens came apparently from Palestine into northern Europe, the Nazi delegation rose and walked out of the room" (*Ibid.*, p. 57). They went straight home and proved there that the Greeks originated in Germany.

Before the First World War, G. Kossinna had claimed Jutland as the cradle of the much-disputed Indo-European parent stock. From Jutland, we are told, this race and culture spread right to the Aegean and the Caucasus. But this theory was short-lived for, as V. Gordon Childe wrote: "German prehistorians, since the 'Versailles Dictate' detached South Jutland from the Reich, have preferred to transfer the cradle . . . of the Indo-Europeans to the more thoroughly Germanic soil of Saxo-Thuringia!" (*The Dawn of European Civilization,* p. 172).

Other countries pride themselves on having been discovered, founded, or colonized by the Greeks, or at least having traded with them, selling them amber or tin. Not so the Herrenvolk: the Greeks were made in Germany. If of Greek literature only Plato's *Republic* had survived, one could not deny the probability of the postulate.

In Saxo-Thuringia a lot of corded ware was found, a type of Neolithic pottery decorated with cord impressions. From the scattered distribution of these pots, German prehistorians concluded that it proved the movement of the Ur-Indo-Germans from Germany to Greece and the Caucasus. They handed this Ariadne cord to Hitler, who followed it in every direction.

But apart from these Nazi insanities, in Germanic
minds Greece has always caused extraordinary brainstorms,
followed by downpours of the most exalted hogwash.
I was fortunate enough to receive wholesome antidotes in early
childhood. It was my grandmother's sister Friederike,
called Tante Fritze, who started the treatment. After an accident
in her thirties, she was bedridden for the rest of her
long life. According to the family this was a blessing, as it saved
her from ending up somewhere on the barricades.
She never was a feminist, but she had other hair-raising ideas.
"Don't listen to her," I was told, and I pricked
up my ears. She detested the growing German mystique,
but consternated the Slavophile and the Germanophile factions
of the family alike by declaring that the European races,
all of them, were degenerate ex-Asiatics, badly in
need of a shot of new blood: "Look at Pushkin!"
And I got the impression that it was the blood of Hannibal,
Pushkin's African grandfather, that not only made Pushkin
a genius but somehow rolled in the veins of every

Russian genius after him. My father detested all factions. "I am Human!" he said, and went shooting or fishing.

Belonging to this more than doubtful Northern race, I have come to refer to it as Maglemosian rather than Nordic. I am a daughter of Maglemosian Forest Folk, those backwoods people who led a hunting and fishing existence from Pre-Boreal times (roughly 7500 B.C.) in an area called most appropriately the Baltic Depression. In the Ice Age, we are told, the Baltic Depression was covered with ice, had an icy outlet into the likewise ice-covered Arctic, and was called "the Yoldia Sea." When the thaw came, it was slightly brackish and was called "Ancylus Lake." Getting Boreal and very salty, it is named "Litorina Sea." And here somewhere the Maglemosians come in.

Gordon Childe, again, has some interesting pertinences in his *The Dawn of European Civilization:* "Certainly by Boreal times, the Forest folk had spread all over the still unbroken *North European plain from Southern England to Finland,* and had achieved a very nice adjustment to their environment of pine woods, interrupted only by lakes and rivers" (p. 9). This nice adjustment, achieved in the Middle Stone Age, is called Maglemosian. Typical Maglemosian equipment has been found on the Baltic shores and in the Urals, and the battle about the origin of the Maglemosians is still going on, not without chauvinistic overtones. No matter where they came from, the population of the European forest zone was far from being homogeneous. "By Sub-Boreal times," writes Childe, "Mongoloid, Lappoid, Europoid and hybrid types are represented in the graves" (p. 203).

There goes the Nordic myth! After the unification of Germany in 1871, the new Empire could afford a new myth, and enthusiastic Teutons, befuddled by Wagner and in utter disregard of facts, obligingly brewed the requested myth. This unfortunate myth, the Nordic Myth, took root in benighted heads, yielded monstrous fruit under the Nazis, and led to World War II. And it still has its resurrections in deranged brains on both sides of the Atlantic.

Ever since the discovery of the Indo-European language group in the late eighteenth century, the purely linguistic term "Indo-European" had been increasingly used or rather misused in an ethnic sense, denoting a hypothetical race vastly superior to any other races. This romantic concept of an Indo-European top race has kept on raising weird chauvinistic bubbles in quite a few "white" brains. In Professor Toynbee's sarcastic words: "A race which had brought forth the religious genius of Zarathustra and the Buddha, the artistic genius of Greece, the political genius of Rome, and—fitting climax—our noble selves! Why, this race was responsible for practically all the achievements of human civilizations" (*A Study of History*, abridged ed., p. 53). Not to forget the ultimate achievements: the Third Reich and the Bomb. And nothing could show the inferiority of the Orientals better than the gunpowder episode: the Chinese had invented it long before the Europeans did. But, instead of making any proper use of it, these primitives used it for fireworks, for fun. How can such people be expected to believe in peaceful co-existence with us?

After all these heady Indo-European draughts, it is a sobering exercise to recall a few achievements of the comparatively small group of Semitic races, who produced Sargon, Hammurabi, Moses, Jesus, Mohammed, Marx, Einstein, and Freud. Forty-three hundred years ago, Sargon was the first to unite city-states of diverse races by conquest into an empire, thereby setting an example for all empire builders from antiquity to the present day. The by-product of these forcible enterprises we call civilizations. Almost four thousand years ago, Hammurabi laid down a code which expressed the idea of justice based on something like a common law instead of force and favor. Moses started the surviving monotheisms, and Jesus Christ, Christianity. Mohammed started Islam, and Marx, Marxism. Trying to shake the Western proletariat into class consciousness, Marx had an unexpected windfall in the East. Thus the ideologies from Moses to Marx in their totality now cover the whole of Europe, the two Americas, Australia, the greater part of Asia and Africa. And since Einstein finally found out what is the matter with matter, and Freud, what is the matter with father, it looks as if these men, from Sargon to Freud, had not only created but also solved every problem we ever had since 2300 B.C.

Nevertheless, after the discovery of the Hurrians, the Hittites, and the Mitanni, and after the decipherment of their scripts, some champions of Indo-Europeanism enthusiastically declared the whole of Anatolia, the Levant, and North Africa as virtually Indo-European territory, Semitic in language only. We had better rely on the authority of Albright: "The dominant bony structure and skull form of the purest known Hamitic and Semitic tribes of today already appear in the Mesolithic of Palestine, nearly ten thousand years ago. Without denying that there were movements of non-Semitic peoples across Palestinean soil between that date and the third millennium B.C., it seems only reasonable to suppose that the Semitic element has remained primary in the ethnic makeup of Palestine ever since" (*Archaeology of Palestine,* pp. 179–80).

Towards the end of the third millennium B.C., the Hurrians obviously moved in from Northern Mesopotamia and became the upper class of Palestine, says Albright. Their language resembled Sumerian and Turkish more than Semitic or Indo-European, but was not related to any of them. These Hurrians have been a noticeable stratum in the ethnic structure of southwestern Asia for nearly a thousand years, but always under the foreign leadership of Hittites, Kassites, or Hyksos. A strictly upper-middle-class race, it seems. From the seventeenth century B.C., their overlords were the Indo-European-speaking Mitanni. In the ethnic upheaval of the twelfth century B.C., these peoples were reshuffled or replaced by newcomers, but the substratum had obviously remained Semitic all the time. The twelfth-century Mycenean tombs of Ugarit, the ancient Phoenician town, show, according to Henri Frankfort, predominantly Semitic names, quite a few Hurrian, and a scattering of Kassite.

"Mesopotamia is ill-defined" is the lapidary opening line of Frankfort's *Art and Architecture of the Ancient Orient.* How true! And how true of every single country in the Near East from antiquity to the present day. To say when, where, how, and why one country ends and the next begins is beyond me, and to cut tiresome arguments about Phoenicia and Canaan short, we had better refer to Albright again. Speaking of the Ugarit texts of 1400 B.C. he concludes: "All these epics can be shown from their contents to have originated in the heart of Canaanite culture, that is, in Phoenicia."

Now the Greeks are still missing in the Levantine picture. The glory that was Greece did not arrive ready-made when they emerged in history. They had been slowly hatched in the Levantine incubator. First known as the Achaeans, they appear in the Aegean as martial hordes of patriarchal he-men and came in waves during the second millennium B.C. The first ones fell under the spell of the old world—in this case, the Minoan—and fashioned their own New Crete in Mycenae. Around 1200 B.C. the last wave, the Dorians, put an end to all that. And right they were, for the big-boned Achaeans must have looked absurd in Minoan attire. The Cretans had traded with them, had invented a simplified script for the illiterate invaders, and finally left the island to them. Quite a few of the Cretans went back to the Levantine coasts; others obviously went straight to Andalusia, taking with them their bull cult, their dances, their flounced skirts, and their slim-waisted men.

The Achaeans arrive in Greece and Anatolia "with nothing but a beautiful language" and absorb everything in their path. Whatever they can lay hands on, they grasp, and under their transmuting touch everything becomes Greek in the end, even the Pillars of Hercules. Gods they create in their own image or, rather, they refashion other people's gods in their own image, and the Olympian pantheon is a mirror of their social structure and struggle and their code of morals, which is not high but attractive. "They were late in learning the alphabet and found the lesson difficult," said Josephus. The result, however, is Greek literature. It started on the Asiatic shore of Greece, and the Levantine incubator remains palpable, as for instance when Herodotus states that Thales, the first Greek philosopher, was of

Phoenician origin. Or when we find in the whole Stoa but one Greek, Kleanthes.

As vase painters, the Greeks are superb. As sculptors too, up to the destruction of Athens. Then they reach the astonishing perfection in reproducing nature, called Classical Style, that becomes the sacrosanct ideal and artistic canon of the Western middle class down to the present day—Plato's *mimesis* theory come true. Copied by the Romans and revived in the Renaissance, this classic-ridden tradition has limited our range of perception so successfully that most people are unable to recognize and appreciate any other art on earth. Which is not the Greeks' fault. However, what a place the Athens of Pericles and Plato must have been! Brilliant and vile, ringing with rhetoric, with a democracy based on slavery and the suppression of women, with pederasty on a pedestal, and all this too-classical art. Original thought was suspect and had to be punished accordingly by hemlock or exile. Two ways were open to original thinkers: to seek refuge abroad or in metaphysics, incomprehensible to the Agora. But when their stocks and stones, the *sacra* of the pre-Greek world, were defiled, all Athens was shaken.

Coming to think of the actual situation behind all the demonstrative façades, one cannot help seeing in Periclean Athens the classical Potemkin Village of antiquity, which in fact it was meant to be. According to Thucydides, Athens "looks twice as powerful as in fact it is." The visible splendor was meant to impress on her allies and the Persians a power she actually did not have. Unruly and unable to rule, the Greeks have supplied posterity with glorious theories telling us how to rule, and our admiration for their tremendous orations knows no bounds.

Tante Fritze gave me an early warning. "Don't be fooled by Plato," she said. "He is a darn swaggerer." It took me a lifetime to find out how well she had read her Plato.

Apropos Two

IT WAS a hundred years ago that an immensely learned Swiss, J. J. Bachofen, discovered the vast substratum underlying our patriarchal history, society, and religion: matriarchy. Although this term and others he coined were misnomers, and although most of his books remained unread, he opened a door that allowed us a new insight into prehistory, anthropology, and religion. Today, after an interregnum of the wildest and most romantic conjectures, it has become almost a truism that there has been a cultural stratum with marked social and religious preponderance of women, that the Father-God was preceded by a Mother-Goddess. (For the best information on this subject, the interested reader should not miss Professor E. O. James's *Cult of the Mother-Goddess,* a marvel of scholarship and wisdom.)

Apparently, the woman had considerable magical power and social prestige during the age of total ignorance. Since the facts of life were not known, she was considered as the sole creatrix of life, and inheritance passed through the female line only, though inheritance belongs properly to the age of semi-ignorance, which is our present age. The shifting of power was not solely a question of property, however. I have a hunch that the female had abused her power as vicaress of the Goddess, just as the male a few thousand years later abused his as vicar of God. And, as the Old Testament points out, it also was a question of knowledge. It was Eve's original sin to let Adam have a share in the apple of knowledge. This bite of knowledge turned the Male's head and Woman lost her original status. As soon as writing starts in Sumer, already we meet a marked antifeminine undercurrent in literature.

The Bible's and the Christian Fathers' resentment against Woman is sufficiently known. So is the Greeks'. But to find it in the Gilgamesh epos surprised me. Whatever and however complex the reasons, this attitude seems to be the result of the great Neolithic revolution: agriculture and husbandry. Instead of gathering the food, women started growing it, which led to controlled food supply. In the long run, this innovation brought greater security, but also restriction of movement, private property, law, marriage, and government—enough to be resentful about. Agriculture made Man sedentary, housebound, a husband.

The Gilgamesh myth is a beautiful and moving illustration. Gilgamesh is dissatisfied with this whole world of the city-state around him, and, in a misogynous mood, starts serious trouble. To distract him, the gods give him a companion "who is like him." Enkidu, the untamed hairy brute, is lured by a Sacred Woman from the savage freedom of wild life with the animals, and domesticated by her for community life. But he does not sleep well on carpets—in fact, I do not know of another epic where heroes sleep so often and so badly—and he is nostalgic for the lost paradisal co-existence with the animals. Gilgamesh joins him, and both sport a wild resentment against Woman. They decide not to beget children in the temple of Ishtar, but do heroic deeds together. And we see the two muscle-men—the prototype of many a Hercules—depicted on countless cylinder seals. But contact with civilization has done Enkidu no good: his sleep deteriorates even more, and he falls ill and dies on a carpet, deeply lamented by Gilgamesh. It is his own animal nature that is gone, and in his lamentations the Beast becomes the Beauty.

As for the Greeks: not even the combined effort of the nine Muses could kindle any enthusiasm for agriculture and women in Hesiod. And not because he is a farmer and knows that farming is not all jam and roses, but first of all because he is Hesiod, who cannot encourage anybody about anything. This is his delightful way of giving advice! "If the desire for uncomfortable seafaring seize you . . . ," he starts his chapter on sailing (*Erga* 618). And "If you ever turn your misguided heart towards trading . . . ," the one on commerce (646). According to Hesiod, Pandora was made on Zeus' request in anger: "Of her is the deadly race and tribe of women, who lived amongst mortal men to their great trouble" (*Theogony* 591). They are "a plague to men who eat bread" (*Erga* 82). And for the farmer he has an extra warning: "Do not let a flaunting woman coax and cozen and deceive you—she is after your barn" (373). That the barn had originally been hers was already forgotten in Hesiod's time.

The Old Testament shows the familiar old grudge: Woman is to be blamed for Man's expulsion from the paradisal state of an existence in sheer ignorance. Without Woman he would have wallowed under the tree of knowledge with the animals forever, without thinking of apples, in an Eden which knew not agriculture. In the story of the Fall we find the nomad's natural disdain for agriculture, which leads him to the sedentary life he did not want. The seminomadic Israelites obviously considered agriculture as a punishment. Man was expelled from Eden and condemned to till the ground, especially cursed by God for the occasion (Gen. 3:17–19). God also showed explicit preference for Abel's meat offering, while for Cain's farm products "he had no respect." Consequently "Cain was very wroth," slew Abel, was cursed by God, gave up farming, and went city-building (4:17).

Not a word more is heard about agriculture until Noah is born, and then what is said has no enthusiastic ring. "This same," says his father Lamech, "shall comfort us concerning our work and toil of our hands, because of the ground which the

Lord has cursed." But somehow everything had got out of hand by now and was in a mess, and God decided to drown this whole creation of his, though he had been so pleased while making it. Only Noah's family and everything else in the ark survived. After the flood "the Lord said in his heart, I will not again curse the ground any more for man's sake" (Gen. 8:21).

But Noah went vine-growing and got drunken and disorderly in rapid succession (Gen. 9:20–1). When he "awoke from his wine" and learned that his son Ham had seen him drunken, he put a curse on Ham's son Canaan, "a servant of servants shall he be unto his brethren," thus legitimizing future claims on the land of Canaan.

This curse of Noah's immortalizes the archetype of truly drunken reasoning, and thus could not fail to become the pivot of racial segregation. When the European powers colonized the globe and needed manpower to do the work in the newly conquered lands, the Christian nations readily fell back on Noah's way of reasoning, and declared that the Negroes, as sons of Ham, were slaves by the will of God, which is patently untrue. For God makes, in Genesis 9, an explicit covenant with Noah *and his sons,* blesses them all, and leaves the stage.

The curse is just a disgruntled outburst of Noah's, arising from the depth of a primeval hangover, and the accursed is Canaan and not Ham. It is an aetiological myth, meant to justify the conquest of Canaan for posterity. And this is how Canaan became the Promised Land.

Apropos Three

THIS LAND of Canaan had been promised in turn to Abraham, to Isaac, and to Jacob. None of them stayed long: they all left for Egypt or Mesopotamia or both, either fleeing famine or obeying a parental request to go abroad and look for marriageable cross-cousins. So their attempts to settle permanently in Canaan had failed.

They failed until Joshua. According to tradition, Moses is the lawgiver and the inaugurator of Monotheism. To establish this new religion and cultus, and to secure religious and political allegiance, Moses, for forty years, kept in the isolation of the desert the composite ethnic body that later entered Canaan as the Hebrews. (It seems that, today, forty years is still considered as the optimal period for effective mass indoctrination.)

For the necessary religious and social drill, Moses chose a megalithic sanctuary at Sinai (Exod. 24:4). And his lawgiving was in the strict tradition of the second millennium B.C. Hammurabi, Minos, and Moses, the lawgivers of Babylonia, Crete, and Palestine, conversed with their respective godheads "on a mountain."

The demonstrative exodus had been of tremendous importance for Israel and, Moses hoped, had duly impressed Egypt. At least, "What will the Egyptians say?" still mattered greatly to him on Sinai. Amid thunder and lightning, the numinous portents of godheads, he was given the commandments, the constitution, and diverse ordinances. To the priestly garments for Aaron and his sons minute attention was paid, down to the "linen breeches to cover their nakedness." All this took time, and the Hebrews, being left alone with Aaron, got bored, and so had the first of their numerous "backslidings" into bull worship, the universal religion during the Bronze and Iron Ages from Egypt to the Euxine and from India to Spain. Yahweh was up against very heavy odds.

So fierce was his wrath about the backsliding that
again he wanted to do away with these creatures of his. But this,
pleaded Moses, would make a most unfavorable
impression on the Egyptians. Yahweh's political prestige was
at stake, for the Egyptians would say: "Because the Lord
was not able to bring them into the land he
promised them, he hath brought them out to slay
them in the wilderness" (Deut. 9:28) .

Yahweh softened, and Moses descended from the Mount.
But when he saw the chosen people, including Aaron,
dancing in the nude round the golden calf, he threw
the tables with the commandments to the winds and
gave rein to the Yahweh in him: three thousand were massacred.
The Deuteronomist is silent about the event.
The Apostle Paul is not, however; but for some reason or other
he makes it "three and twenty thousand" (I Cor. 10:7–8) .

Later we hear of the Israelites backsliding with monotonous frequency. One cannot blame them. Being the chosen people of an all-transcending god was not only a crushing burden, but made them objectionable misfits all around. They were under the religious obligation *not* to co-operate or fraternize with other peoples. By their uncompromising Apartheid—for this is surely the first documented case of Apartheid in history—the Hebrews excluded themselves from the commonwealth of nations. And thus a tragedy singular on earth began.

Politically the Hebrews were a failure. They were bound to be. (What an absurd idea, to settle a small ethnic group right in the middle of the Near Eastern thoroughfare towards the end of the second millennium B.C. To promise a land then and there! And "forever," a word so dear to gods and lovers!) But Moses and the Prophets were fully able to justify that: it was only the people's backsliding that caused the political failure. In this way an endlessly pervading sense of shortcoming and guilt was evoked and manipulated. They were utterly worthless before God, they were told, but, being the chosen people, still vastly superior to all other nations. Here we find what Henri Frankfort called "a new and utter lack of *eudaemonia,* of harmony—whether with the world of reason or with the world of perception." Frankfort refined his evaluation by saying "nowhere else do we meet this fanatical devaluation of the phenomena of nature and the achievements of man: art, virtue, social order—in view of the unique significance of the divine" (*Before Philosophy,* pp. 245, 243) .

Even after they have finally fought their way from Sinai over the Jordan into Canaan, they are told that this has nothing to do with military qualifications or any other human endeavor; far from it: "I delivered them into your hand, and I sent the hornet before you, which drave them out from before you, even the two kings of the Amorites; *but not with thy sword, nor with thy bow"* (Josh. 24:11–12) .

This distinction is made through the mouth of Joshua; and, in case they do not yet feel deep enough in the red, Yahweh continues: "And I have given you a land for which ye did not labour, and cities which ye built not, and ye dwell in them; of the vineyards and oliveyards which ye planted not do ye eat. Now therefore fear the Lord and serve him in sincerity and in truth: and put away the gods which your fathers served on the other side of the flood, and in Egypt; and serve ye the Lord" (24:13–14) .

At the gates of Canaan, the zone of agriculture, it became

evident that without displaying all the faculties of the fertility-Baalim around him, Yahweh for all his transcendence had no chance. A god who cannot give or withhold rain is no success in an agrarian land. Canaan, the Deuteronomist points out, "is not as the land of Egypt from whence ye came out, where thou sowedst it with thy hand, as a garden of herbs. But the land whither ye go to possess it is a land of hills and valleys, and drinketh water of the rain of heaven" (11:10–11). Palestine has no great rivers like Egypt or Mesopotamia, but depends entirely on rain. So Yahweh becomes the "rider upon the heaven" and the rider "upon a swift cloud" (Deut. 33:26; Ps. 68:4; Isa. 19:1), as Baal had been "rider upon the cloud" in the fourteenth-century B.C. Ugarit texts, and Enlil in Mesopotamia the "rider upon great storms" still earlier. And finally, he holds the rain monopoly in the Old Testament.

At the gates of the promised land the tribes of Israel hear for the last time the great evocative voice of Moses. After the familiar deafening volley of curses and blessings, follows Yahweh's promise: "My doctrine shall drop as rain, my speech shall distill as the dew, as the small rain upon the tender herb and as the shower upon the grass."

What an appropriate metaphor in the face of Canaan!
But doctrine does not help the crops.

The book of Joshua is a report of conquest and war, and as such inevitably bloodthirsty. War is as beastly in the Bible as in the Iliad or the Edda, and biblical victory songs are like all victory songs: boastful, sanguinary, muscular, inaccurate, and embarrassing. "So Joshua smote all the country of the hills, and of the south, and of the vale, and of the springs, and all their kings: he left none remaining, but utterly destroyed all that breathed, as the Lord God of Israel commanded" (Josh. 10:40). The Israelites had been commanded to do so, but did nothing of the sort. "The extermination of the Canaanites from Palestine was miraculous, but incomplete," as the "Historical Summary" of the Sunday School Teacher's Edition of the Holy Bible puts it. Had they utterly destroyed all that breathed, there would have been nobody left to teach them agriculture and do the work in Canaan.

Apropos Four

"MEN MAKE GODS and women worship them," says Sir James Frazer. Strabo thinks that, left to himself, man would never have got the idea of worship. There is something to it: without the lush fertility rites with goddesses and the sacred marriage, the puritanical Yahweh would probably never have occurred to Moses.

According to the Bible, it is the women who make men "go a-whoring after gods." They went a-whoring throughout the whole Old Testament, before David established Yahwism in Jerusalem under the united monarchy in the tenth century; they continued under the double kingdom until the time of Jeremiah in the sixth century, and even after the captivity they went on a-whoring: "My people ask counsel at their stocks and their staff declareth unto them: for the spirit of whoredoms hath caused them to err, and they have gone a-whoring from under their God. They sacrifice upon the tops of the mountains, and burn incense upon the hills, under oaks and poplars and elms, because the shadow thereof is good: therefore your daughters shall commit whoredom, and your spouses shall commit adultery" (Hos. 4:12–13).

What extraordinary language and metaphors! The prophets knew what they were talking about, and in most cases their language is far from metaphorical. Led badly astray into Puritanism by our Judeo-Christian tradition, we can hardly comprehend what these biblical authors are talking about. They are talking about contemporary religion, and their metaphors are neither metaphors nor farfetched.

To face this, we must descend from the heights of our puritan morals and enter the realm of ancient fertility religion. *The Book of Beasts,* T. H. White's translation of a twelfth-century bestiary, recommends for such adventures the example of the ibex, which when hurled down from great heights never comes to any harm, but always lands on its strong and shock-resistant horns: "The Ibex symbolizes learned men, who are accustomed to shock-absorb whatever adversities befall them with a harmonization of the two Testaments, as if with some protecting braking-action."

I am not a learned man, but a curious old woman, who,
after a long life on rather moral heights, now at last can enjoy
reading the Bible at the foot of the Pillars of Hercules. My
upbringing was just average puritan, and in no way
exceptional. My father never separated the rooster from the
hens on Sunday, as puritan farmers still do.
Nevertheless, it was an anemic age; but during my lifetime,
through the endeavor of anthropology, archaeology,
and other new sciences, the tree of knowledge has yielded an
abundance of excellent fruit; we have eaten to the
great benefit of our "psychometabolism," and our eyes have been
opened as never before.

And now let us enter the Promised Land. There were the agricultural Canaanites with their fertility rites, in their heathen innocence playing the harlot under every green tree, never having heard of Original Sin. These pagans enjoyed a guiltless sex life, which was integrated into their religion in a perfectly natural manner. Mating was a cult observance in their ritual, at times restricted, at times encouraged, with the blessing and for the benefit of the Church, for the good of the community, for the welfare of the State.

To the ancient agriculturalist, deeply involved in nature, such phenomena of life as procreation and fertility were manifestations of the gods. The perennial recurrent growth and decay of vegetation, and the cyclic recurrence of mating and bearing in the animal kingdom, demanded man's best attention, veneration, and active assistance. The continuation of these phenomena on which the existence of the community ultimately depended was of the deepest communal concern. Man shares with many animals an urge for ritual, for frills. Just ploughing, planting, and sowing was not enough for the emotional needs of the community: to induce and secure crops and offspring more things had to be done, and thus "things done," *dromena*, started, and the whole string of sympathetic magic. From Sir James Frazer, Jane E. Harrison, Malinowsky, and others, we know about the origin, function and significance of incantations, songs, dances, and pantomimes that formed the strictly formalized ritual of agricultural festivals, accentuating the ploughing, sowing, growing, harvesting, and storing.

The cycle of agricultural rites revolved around the Dying God and the *Hieros Gamos,* the Sacred Marriage. From time immemorial it has been the thing done, the *dromenon,* indispensable in fertility ritual. At the beginning of the agricultural year the sanctity of procreation had to be demonstrated, and king and queen, or other priestly functionaries, performed the sacred marriage of the gods, the *Hieros Gamos.* This ritual is older than agriculture and older than marriage. In fact our form of marriage grew out of this ritual, and quite a few terms of conjugal legislation are based on agricultural jargon, as the word "conjugal" shows. It means "yoked together."

What splendid self-confidence the Primitive displays in doing magic! It is his doing that makes the grass grow green, and it is his religious duty to encourage the birds and the bees by demonstration.

This ritual met the disapproval of the prophets and embarrassed the Greeks, who drove it literally underground, did it in darkness only, and called it a "Mystery." This was a

grievous mistake and caused a lot of obscure and pious
humbug. But mystery religions became the trend of the time,
Orphism was made the state religion of Athens, and
concepts like sin and vengeance crept in. Orphic eschatological
means were rather subtle, however, and they
never made much of Hades. Not that the Greeks were too
civilized to raise hell—real Hell, originating in Persia, became a
Christian achievement—but their religion was not much
concerned with it. About the worst that could happen to you
after death was "to sit in mud" in ill-lit Hades forever.
It is only on second thought that this cheerless prospect takes
on a nightmarish quality, comparable to Saint
Teresa's vision of Hell. She saw a dark narrow passage, the
ground a cold mud. It was so dark that she could
only just see at the end of the passage a cupboard, and crammed,
cramped into that cupboard—herself. What a cool vision,
while all Christendom was ablaze with human bonfires!

The Greeks got their mysteries from Crete, where they were
not mysteries. Ritual mating was a *dromenon* but no "mystery."
Diodorus informs us that the rites practiced by the Athenians at
Eleusis "are celebrated darkly and mystically; but in Crete, at
Cnossos, by ancient law, the very same sacred mysteries are celebrated plainly and openly, and whatever is done in secret by
others, none amongst them conceals from any that have the desire to know them" (V. 4).

The Greeks concealed, and the initiates kept a strict arcane
discipline. This was altogether maddening to the Christian
Fathers, when later they were to establish a mystery religion of
their own. Nearly all we know about the Greek Mysteries we
owe to the indefatigable curiosity of these "reverend Christian
scandal-mongers," as Frazer called them. With a little detachment one can greatly enjoy their apoplectic rage against
Woman, and how, in their obsessional negative preoccupation
with sex, they have a go at the sacred marriage. Only to find out
that, like the Jews before them, they could not do without it.

Apropos Five

To the Greeks all other gods are like theirs. To the Jews no other god is like Theirs. According to the generally entertained tradition, he is the all-transcending God. This all-transcending God leaves the phenomenal world only gradually. He retains all human properties except one: shape. From Egypt to Canaan he is visible to his people as a pillar of cloud by day and a pillar of fire by night (Exod. 13:21–22). Once at dawn, when the pillars were changing watch, "the Lord looked unto the host of the Egyptians through the pillar of fire and of cloud, and troubled the host of the Egyptians" (14:24). I must admit, those pillars also troubled me. I met them unexpectedly, and they came to me almost as a shock.

This God becomes manifest and grows in the course of a dramatic experience in history: the rise and fall of a small and passionate nation, whose claim on a Near Eastern territory has gained a unique significance only in retrospect, while it went unnoticed at the time when all lands, cities, thrones, and victories were promised by gods. Since in the wider historical context of the Near East this small nation has no political importance, we hardly hear of them in contemporary annals, except their own. They are unknown to Herodotus, who has an ethnologist's ear and eye for the extraordinary, and who knew Palestine.

Nevertheless, as we have seen, in this small Semitic nation originated four of the world's prominent ideologies: Yahwism, Christianity, Islam, and Marxism. All four are violently opposed to one another and exclude one another absolutely, because they are based on the same principle: the totalitarian One-God-Only principle. Tolerant monotheism is a contradiction in terms.

The Arabs, in greatness of expansion comparable only to
the Romans before them and the Mongols after them,
conquered in the name of their God, who was the God of
Abraham and repeatedly had promised Abraham: "Unto thy
seed will I give this land" (Gen. 12:7).

It is not the first and not the last time that Yahweh has got
himself into a quandary, for Ishmael is of Abraham's
seed, and Ishmael and Isaac are brothers. And there they are,
the same brothers in the same setting of Canaan,
having created a similar situation all over again in the middle
of the twentieth century!

For over two thousand years the Chinese, Buddhists, Greeks, and Christians have been preaching the Brotherhood of Man, and for much longer than that we have kept on proving how this brotherhood works *de facto*, and are bewailing the sad fact. But if we look at biblical brothers, they are a hostile and sad lot, and we had better face it: in biblical myth the first man born on this earth was a murderer. It is a wise myth and a horrible one.

We do not believe any longer in murder as free enterprise, but we have sanctioned mass murder as war. And the fifth commandment, "Thou shalt not kill," should be supplemented, "unless there is a war on."

What is it that made and makes men go to the wars? Need and greed, boredom, aggression, vandalism, ideologies, vanity, and prestige. And there will always be a pretext. The Greeks made Helen the pretext of their Trojan War. It was a lovely pretext, but was not taken seriously by their own historians, and was rightly discarded as a cause by Herodotus (2. 113–20). In his record of Croesus' conquests, Herodotus starts frankly with the cause: "He coveted the land, which he wished to add to his own dominion"; but knowing his readers who always want to recognize a god's finger in their war-pies, he hastens to add an interminable pretext: "But the chief reason . . . ," a story going back to an oracle given by the Pythoness five generations before, showing how the whole matter had been predestined by Apollo (1.13, 73–91).

For the conquest of Canaan the Israelites had to go back quite a few more generations for a pretext: the pretext that the land had been made over to them as an inheritance in a covenant by their God, who was the God of Abraham; and they took their pretext seriously. So did the Arabs; for had not their God, who was the God of Abraham, said after the birth of Ishmael: "I will give unto thee and to thy seed after thee the land wherein thou art a stranger, all the land of Canaan, for an everlasting possession; and I will be their God" (Gen. 17:8)? The priestly writer tries hard to cope with this commitment God has made in his wild generosity. But the Arabs too, taking their God seriously, insist upon their everlasting covenant.

I wish people would take neither themselves nor their gods too seriously, for it brings out the worst in us, as we have sufficiently proved. And so we end up with the most absurd situation: we have Yahwism, Christianity, and Islam, the three Monotheistic creeds, stemming from the same root, revealed and divided by the same God! Their attitude towards one another was summed up by Gibbon in a footnote in his sixth volume: "Among the Arab philosophers Averroës has been accused of despising the religion of the Jews, the Christians and the Mohammedans. Each of these sects would agree that in two instances out of three this contempt was reasonable."

In the name of Allah, the God of their patriarch Abraham, the Arabs conquered the world from Malaya to the Atlantic. They destroyed comparatively little, and never on the biblical

"destroy utterly" principle; for they had learned, first from
the Persians and later from the Romans, that it does not pay
to destroy the conquered—better tax them. Our history books
call this a refinement in the arts of war. The juvenile
vandalism of "destroy utterly" gave way to a more mature and
reflective mood: conquer, loot, but do not devastate and
kill more than necessary, for the dead cannot profit you.
It is by far more profitable to let people live, make them work
for you, and tax them. Or as Churchill, appropriately
more civilized, put it in a minute of April 1, 1945:
"The so-called 'area bombing' of German cities should be
reviewed from the point of view of our own interests. If we come
into control of an entirely ruined land, there will be a great
shortage of accommodation for ourselves and our allies."

It was something similar, pragmatic reflections rather than
humane spirit, that made the Arabs' conquest of Spain
comparatively bloodless and caused the Caliph Omar to say:
"We must live on our Christians and our descendants
must live on theirs, as long as Islam lasts." For this reason too,
the Caliphate did not encourage conversion, for the
Christians were highly taxed and every convert would
have meant sheer loss to the treasury. And for another and by
now familiar reason it seemed advisable not to destroy utterly:
the Arab's disdain for agriculture. This despised activity
was better left to the natives.

I wonder how the Phoenicians behaved in Spain and elsewhere. Although they introduced and spread the alphabet,
hardly any of their own records have come down to us, besides
their Pillars of Hercules and a few bills: as for instance the
tablet in Marseilles, a Greek colony, telling us how much the
priests of Baal charged for a sacrifice. Or the report in II Maccabees 4:19, where the high priest Jason sends three hundred
drachmae to the temple of Hercules in Tyre for the Melkarth
festival. They had peculiar worshiping habits, as will be seen
later, but one fact remains unchallenged: the Phoenicians did

not believe in making wars, and also refused to sail with the Persians against their own kin, herewith displaying an extravagant sentiment unknown to Jews and Greeks. They also did another thing that looked absurd to "conquerors": they paid rent to the Berbers for the territory of Carthage.

The Phoenicians believed in business. And had no ax to grind. Which makes them an oasis in the desert of hypocrisy where Divine Rights are claimed to justify conquest. And I deeply sympathize with the indignation felt by a French historian towards the Spanish conquest of Mexico and Peru: "Without all this religious ideology which, in their eyes, legitimized their violence, they would have been nothing more than mere brigands, murderers, and highwaymen. The invaders brandished Bulls and theological texts, a whole rubbish-heap of documents, by way of justifying their invasion" (Louis Bertrand and Charles Petrie, *The History of Spain,* p. 182).

These harsh words only echo the sentiment felt by the Canaanites, as documented in a Phoenician inscription on two pillars at Tingis, the African side of the Straits of Hercules. "We are they who fled before the brigand Joshua, son of Nane" (Procopius, *Vandal War* 1. 2. 10). For the brigand's report, read the book of Joshua, who reports almost exclusively victories and no casualties, as war correspondents do.

So far as I know, Herodotus is the first and almost the last historian to display fairness in historical judgment, which is remarkable in a fifth-century Ionian who came to admire Athens greatly. It takes considerable impartiality and fairness to write in the history of these admired Athenians: "There were certain Pelasgians whom the Athenians once drove out of Attica; whether they did it justly or unjustly I cannot say, since I only know what is reported concerning it" (6. 137). At least it was intelligent to take a neutral stand, for there were contemporary historians around who did not side with Athens, like Hecataeus. "The Athenians," according to him, "had given to the Pelasgi a tract of land at the foot of Hymettus as payment for the wall with which the Pelasgians had surrounded their citadel. This land was barren and little worth at the time: but the Pelasgians brought it into good condition; whereupon the Athenians begrudged them the tract and desired to recover it. And so, without any better excuse, they took arms and drove out the Pelasgians" *(Ibid.)*. How very un-Athenian, to take arms without any lengthy preamble by a military orator! "These same Pelasgians, however, . . . conceived the wish to be revenged on the Athenians," and this is the way it goes on in history, Herodotus' or any other.

And this was the way it went on with the Israelites and the native or other peoples who had also chosen Canaan, as for instance the Philistines, who had made the coast of Canaan the land of their choice in the twelfth century B.C.

The Philistines were a tall, good-looking, and hard-drinking people. Their good looks are recorded by the Egyptians and their drinking habits by the Bible. As archaeology shows, they made splendid pottery and after the fall of the Hittites held the iron monopoly. And nearly all the time they were a pain in the neck of Israel. Archaeology also proves that the Philistines did not arrive in Palestine before the twelfth century B.C. This would place Abraham—who, according to Genesis (21:32–3), had dealings with them—*after* the exodus, which is very unlikely.

For lack of records so far, we do not know the name of the god who promised Canaan to the Philistines after they, like the Israelites, had also had negative experiences with Egypt. We must remember that all peoples at all times have waged wars at the request or in the name of their gods. Land was always bestowed by a god or goddess on followers or favorites, as sacred writings from all over prove. It was the universal *casus belli*.

The trouble starts when different gods promise the same land to different peoples; or, more embarrassing, when the same god has promised the same land to different people who will not forget the commitment, as happened also to the Hittites. Hattussilis III and Urhi-Teshub claimed the same throne, promised to both of them by the goddess Ishtar, they said. This hard-working goddess, whose departments were love, fecundity, war, and peace, had absent-mindedly committed herself to both sides. Luckily Hattussilis reminded her in time. "And," he writes, "because my Lady Ishtar had previously promised me the throne, so now she visited my wife in a dream (saying) : I am helping thy husband, and all Hattussas will return to the side of thy husband." Presumably the wife told the husband that the goddess had told her, and Hattussilis had the news immediately noised over the country. This helped, and Hattussilis continues his annals: "Then I saw great favour from Ishtar. She deserted Urhi-Teshub and in none but (her own) city of Samuha she shut him up like a pig in a sty . . . , and all Hattussas returned to me" (O. R. Gurney, *The Hittites,* p. 179) .

This story shows how forgetful gods can be, but also how they can be helped by prayers to remember their commitments. And in case this too fails, Man has the healthy faculty of forgetting in the end.

The Jews never forgot. And this is half their tragedy. They do not want to forget—thus, as they should know by now, neglecting one of the major rules of mental hygiene—but persist in preserving their casuistic self-inflicted suffering, to which the rest of the world responds with a similarly senseless reaction, which is the other half of the tragedy. Like all gods, Yahweh made reckless promises, but not without convincing his followers through the mouth of his prophets that it had been entirely their fault and they were the ones to blame when those promises were not fulfilled. What wholesome arguments with Yahweh the Jews have in Talmudic writings—but in the formative period, in the Pentateuch, hardly ever: until they become as meek as Christians at their worst, feeling best when deepest in the red, like Pascal in his *Pensées,* that melancholy monument to Christian wretchedness. How refreshing it is amidst the stifling lamentations of Jeremiah to hear him change gear: "Righteous art thou, O Lord, when I plead with thee: yet let me reason with thee of thy judgments: wherefore doth the way of the wicked prosper? wherefore are all they happy that deal very treacherously?" (Jer. 12:1). This is just a fleeting moment, however, and the chapter that began in this splendid rebellion ends in the monotonous, all too familiar: "If they will not obey, I will utterly pluck up and destroy that nation, saith the Lord."

The catalogue of sins the prophets endlessly dwell upon is rather small. In fact it is a one-sin catalogue: "And he [one king or another] did that which was evil in the sight of the Lord," or more often: "And the children of Israel went a-whoring," both meaning that they preferred the Canaanite way with stocks and stones and bulls to the worship of Yahweh, which of course is outrageous in the sight of the new Lord, who, the Prophets insist, is the supreme godhead first and the Only True God in the end. "And the children of Israel went a-whoring" becomes the chief leitmotif of the Old Testament, the preamble to every mishap: war, defeat, plague, famine, exile. It becomes the favorite formula of the Prophets, who are so infinitely more concerned with the exaltation and reputation of their God than with his people. "Thou art my battle-axe," cries Yahweh or Jeremiah, who are as usual in such a huddle as to become indistinguishable. But there can be no doubt that the people are battlefield and victim, and it is agonizing to see the Prophets fight and win this battle for their God at the cost of his people. This God is molded in the fiery mind of his champions, who do not hesitate to dedicate and sacrifice the people for God's sake. In their *furor theologicus,* the Prophets blame every misfortune on the Jews, thus unwittingly starting the classical and durable institution of anti-Semitism, which is beyond logic and reason. During this painful process, when every mishap that befalls the people is prefixed *post hoc* with the tag, "and the children of Israel went a-whoring," an almost blameless God gradually emerges, while his people sink into a morass of guilt *ad majorem Dei gloriam.* Which obliged the Jews to repent for more sins than they ever could have committed.

Ezra unfortunately had a very different opinion about the sin of Israel. "Seeing that thou our God hast punished us less than our iniquities deserve," he takes the law into his own hands and starts Apartheid in earnest; and this is the darkest chapter of the Old Testament, because race relations are made the scapegoat for the Israelites' political failure.

I am against hair shirts. And that goes for hair-shirt
wearers of every denomination. It is an unwholesome and
distasteful garment, and discarding it would make the mental
climate of the world much healthier.

There is a lot of sackcloth and ashes in the Old Testament. In the beginning it has a sound dash of "serves you right," then it rises to the enormous accusation that the people's disobedience has caused the disaster, and finally it is turned into the Will of God, the most glorious rationalization of failure.

Apropos Six

As FOR RELIGION: I am all for religions so long as they do not do too much harm, and Christianity has done a lot of harm. But no religion that "works" should be rejected; that is, no religion which does not add to misery but eases it, and does not upset a healthy psychometabolism but restores an upset one.

It is intolerance that gets me. And since my upbringing was more or less Christian, MY intolerance is aroused mostly by the claim of Christianity to have the legitimate monopoly on love, the claim to have been chosen to out-love any other religion. Love has been preached from about 500 B.C. in the Far, Middle, and Near East, and in every language since.

Love has been over-preached to such an extent that I find it an enormous relief and blessing to live at last in a country where even lovers do not say "I love you," but *"te quiero,"* I want you, I desire you, which is more honest. The Spanish language never uses the expression as small currency: it is kept for rare and exalted moments, for poetry. And in no country but Spain have I ever heard at the height of joy, of ecstasy over a perfect song or dance, the exclamation: "Viva Dios!", long live God. He certainly does.
What a stupendous structure Christianity has become,

combining and blending a multitude of styles, fascinating and
beautiful in parts, but with the windows all to one side.
I have spent quite a part of my life in this ponderous,
labyrinthine, and unsanitary edifice that has emerged from a
blueprint of such simplicity.
"In my Father's house are many mansions."

But no plumbing. And so I left, for lack of fresh air.
Living now in a room of my own, with a view on this world.
Enjoying myself immensely with antiques.

Religion is a universal social phenomenon. Rooted in emotion, carried by emotion, religion will presumably last as long as
emotions last in mankind, and change with changing man.

While the old religions were an unconscious, anonymous, and
collective product of mankind, the great movements of the last
millennium B.C. were conceived and consciously inaugurated by
individual and historical men, whose fragmentary biographies
have been wildly overgrown by legends.

As if in a universal surfeit of gods and ritual, there is in these
religious movements a general tendency to sober up, from China
to the Levant. Of these—Confucianism, Buddhism, Zoroastrianism, Moses' Yahwism, and Orphism—it seems that only Confucianism has remained comparatively intact: an admirable
frame of thought and state of mind, but too sober for the multitude, so that opium supplemented the religion of the masses. In
Zoroastrianism, Buddhism, Yahwism, and Christianity, the initial purity of concept was soon impregnated by older elements,
which enter not by force but by osmosis, and stay.

The corpus of Old Testament writings is as rich, bewildering,
and ambiguous as the manifold superimposed graphic
representations of Magdalenian cave art. In this extremely
complex picture we see only the outlines we have been taught
to see by teachers, who have been taught to see by teachers,
and so on back. During the last decades we used to refer to
education behind the Iron Curtain as brainwashing and

indoctrination. Communists are brainwashed: we are educated, which means that we have been brainwashed as children with mental drill, slogans, and tautology until in our bland minds the ruts required by social convention have been formed, in which our trends of thought are supposed to run in the desired way. Which they do, as we all know. And with tenacity we cling to these acquired mental habits, as we find out to our distress whenever we make the effort to become familiar with different modes of thought, whenever we go a-whoring. It is not easy to learn, and so hard to unlearn.

Any change of mental habits, such as religious or political conversions, can be accelerated by systematic deprivation of food, sleep, and, as all prophets from Moses to Mao know, relaxation. Within a single chapter of Jeremiah we get a taste of the method. After having been tossed, bruised, and shaken thoroughly, there is a slowdown to smoothing, soothing loving-kindness, and we begin to relax—only to realize with a jerk that he is back in first gear again.

Pursuing the Pillars of Hercules deep into geography, history, and the Bible, I suddenly became aware of a God I never saw before, which means that I look at him for the first time through grown-up eyes. Why have preachers never told me? By now I should know: indoctrinated by their ideology and dogma, they in turn condition us to grasp only the conventional theological significance of the picture, while all other associations are blocked. And we are left with interpretations of such familiar dullness that we never even try to look at the implicit under-lying and fascinating myth, hidden from us by indoctrination. This is apparently a necessary occupational deficiency of theologians and not their fault, as pointed out by the late Heinrich Zimmer, the brilliant interpreter of Indian myth: "Their outlook on life's ambiguous and ambivalent features is narrowed by their dogmatism. They lack (this is a result of their training) that cynicism and that perilous innocence, candid and childlike, which are basic requirements of anyone dealing with myths. They lack (and this is their virtue, their duty) that touch of 'amorality' which must form part at least of one's intellectual and intuitive pattern, if one is not to fall prey to predetermined bias . . ." (*Myths and Symbols in Indian Art and Civilization*, p. 179, footnote).

In spite of theologians and regardless of belief, the myths of antiquity have lost none of their inspiring power, as modern writings convincingly show. And biblical myths now have a grip on me that they never had while I "believed."

Apropos Seven

LOOKING at the Old Testament this way, I notice in it for the first time the portrait of Yahweh as a young god. Apart from his pillar-epiphany, he is human, exceedingly human. So human, indeed, that at last one begins to understand him. This is not the God of theology, this is the God of Man. His emphasis is on this world, and because he is so much of this world, he is the living God and not the Ultimate Reality of the Other World, for no other world has yet come into his mind. He is the first and only god who asks for our partnership and love, not to be reached through speculation, but through the heart. He is the best God we ever had.

He has not yet created the Church that will get him in the end and reduce him to an Absolute Being. The Greeks have not yet started their Indo-European language game "to be or not to be." This is still solid Bronze Age, free from the metaphysical fog into which his son will be born, to exalt him completely out of this world. This is still Yahweh.

With an engaging lack of omniscience he starts his operations in Genesis. In a truly nomadic "agriculture-be-damned" mood he creates grass, herbs, and trees first and the sun and moon afterwards. And of rain he does not think until after the weekend. Whoever doubts this should read chapters one and two of Genesis. Or better still, the whole Old Testament. It is more ferocious and beautiful than any other book; it is majestic and funny, it is God's autobiography, ghostwritten by Moses and the Prophets.

This is Bible Revisited, and a delightful return it is. For the first time in my life I am able to enjoy the Bible straight, instead of diluted with theology. For this ability to look at the Bible with detached fondness instead of atheistic zeal, I am deeply indebted to an old Prussian general, called Der Alte Dessauer, famous for martial merits also, but mostly for his rudeness and never for his wisdom. Hearing of someone who got upset and ashamed about illusions he had cherished as a young man, old Dessauer said, "Tell him one ought to respect the dreams of one's youth." I love this saying; it reveals more wisdom than meets the eye, and I found it immensely helpful when I began rearranging the interior decoration of my mind. We need not resent the dreams of our youth and discard them as "rubbish." One can find delight in them, as one delights in antiques, family heirlooms, or archaeological finds, and they are just as exciting to come across. In the process of these rummagings we also make finds that make us laugh, for, from our present point of view, they can look incongruous and irresistibly comic. Though we laugh not with contempt or shame, but with amused delight. In Ernest Cassirer's words: "Such is the peculiar character of comic catharsis: things and events begin to lose their weight, scorn is dissolved into laughter and laughter is liberation" (*Essay on Man*, p. 192).

By language and laughter Man becomes the animal of distinction—Homo; and only by laughter at himself and his works and his gods—Homo Sapiens. It is solely when Man looks at himself and this world without a trace of humor and in beastly earnestness that this beautiful world becomes a vale of tears. The beauty is in the eye of the beholder.

The Greeks of Homer had the nerve to see the joke in their gods, who were so much like men. "Of one race, one only are men and gods," wrote Pindar before he lost nerve. They were superior in rank, but were not beyond thunderous blundering, and men laughed at them and were fond of them, as the British are fond of their Royal Family. Although to Thales the world was still full of gods, in his own words, he began wondering what this world was made of. He began observing facts and drawing conclusions, and thus opened the door to early scientific and philosophic inquiry. With him started the belief in the intelligibility of things, nature, and the universe. With him started the great adventure of the human intellect, and the trust in Man's unlimited capacity to know. Two hundred years after Thales, we see in Plato, after Socrates had talked everything to shreds, that this trust in Man was shaken, and that consequently the gods had lost their human nature and form. In their place an *Idea of God* had arisen that was perfect and had nothing in common with Man. To my mind *this* was the Greeks' "failure of nerve," their retreat from reality and escape into metaphysics. At the turn of our era, Gilbert Murray saw the failure of nerve in Greek thought, in their resignation to a more limited human mind, and their admission of realms where "only God knows," until finally knowledge became the prerogative of God.

Nowadays it looks as if we were at last recovering our wits, the nerve that failed the Greeks, and can fondly detect Yahweh's humanity and the divine comedy in the Old Testament, where laughter had not been heard since Abraham. Happily there is a good deal of divine comedy in the Old Testament, next to unspeakable terror.

Apropos Eight

IN CASSIRER'S OPINION, "Prophecy does not mean simply fore-telling." It does not, but it did: it certainly and almost exclusively did mean foretelling to the Apostles, as one look at the New Testament shows. Homer too claimed to know the future. And how we still love having our futures told—whether from tea leaves, cards, crystal balls, palms, or horoscopes! But two or three thousand years ago superstition was even worse than it is today. As if that were not enough, the Prophets planted two new and pernicious shoots right in the middle of this superstitious jungle: sin and guilt, Puritan's delight, which we have been plagued with ever since.

All countries and all ages had their prophets, prophetesses, oracles, and sibyls, uttering more or less inspired utterances, and denouncing one another as crooks. This mudslinging was continued vigorously amongst the Christian Fathers and theologians, and flourishes today most conspicuously amongst politicians and critics.

What are prophets for? Mainly to make up our minds. For nothing can be such a bother as making up one's mind. And here the prophets come in, nowadays the admen and salesmen of State, Church, and Industry. Whether articles

of faith or other articles, effective salesmen can sell anything.
They thrive on our ignorance and indolence, on our
indecision and lack of judgment.

What is prophecy "normally"? If we listen to party leaders
in an election campaign, we know what prophecy is.
Of the same stuff is every Five Year Plan and every program.
Churchill did not need divine inspiration to prophesy that
German cities would be "heaps." That is not to belittle
Churchill or the Prophets, but to dampen our credulity.

During the last millennia B.C., the ancient Near East saw
empires falling in rapid succession: Egypt, Babylonia, Assyria,
Persia, Macedonia, and, just coming in, Rome. And one must
keep in mind that Palestine was constantly part of the theater of
war. So it did not necessarily take divine revelations to foretell
the fall of cities and nations at the time of the Prophets (which
means roughly from Tiglath-pileser III to Alexander, or 730–
330). Rather it suggested itself, became habit-forming, became
an end in itself, and triumphed in apocalyptic rhapsodies carried into Christianity by Saint John.

When Egypt and Babylonia and Assyria got into each other's
hair, Israel and Judah were literally in their way, and the great
powers frequently got the two of them under their feet. Esarhaddon's reign (681–669) will illustrate. He marched into
Egypt—through Palestine; returned victorious—through Palestine; rebuilt Babylon, which had been ruined by his father, and
died on his way to Egypt—through Palestine. He left a good
reputation in Assyrian history, numerous heaps in geography, and
sixty-four curses, excavated and published just recently; very
like the curses in Leviticus, they are, and even more like those in
Deuteronomy. Standard curses of the Semitic Iron Age, it seems.

In 689 B.C. Esarhaddon's father Sennacherib had sacked Babylon in a manner that made his contemporary Isaiah say: "And
Babylon, the glory of kingdoms, the beauty of the Chaldees'
excellency, shall be as when God overthrew Sodom and Gomor-
rah. It shall never be inhabited, neither shall it be dwelt in

from generation to generation . . ." (13:19–22). It did not take
her even one generation to arise again from her heaps in mere-
tricious splendor, the Great Whore, and there was not a king
who did not want to conquer her. In Jeremiah's beautiful
words: "Babylon hath been a golden cup in the Lord's hand
that made all the earth drunken: the nations have drunken of
her wine; therefore the nations are mad" (51:7). But of her resurrections we shall, of course, never hear in her enemies' annals.
Nor do these enemies ever mention that it was Sennacherib who
built the first aqueduct.

The incessant flow of the great powers' armies through Palestine inspired Isaiah with the wishful daydream of seeing them
all united under Israel's hegemony: "In that day shall there be
a highway out of Egypt to Assyria, and the Assyrian shall come
into Egypt, and the Egyptian into Assyria; and the Egyptians
shall serve with the Assyrians. In that day shall Israel be the
third with Egypt and with Assyria, even a blessing in the midst
of the land: whom the Lord of hosts shall bless, saying, Blessed
be Egypt my people, and Assyria the work of my hands, and
Israel mine inheritance" (19:23–5). A splendid idea, though
most unorthodox. But Isaiah went unheard, and they are still at
each other's throats. The Deutero-Isaiah makes an even more
unorthodox move: he makes Cyrus an honorary anointed one,
anointed by Yahweh *in absentia;* which is about as far as he can
go with him. This king cannot be called to heel, as Samuel had
done with Saul, for Cyrus not only is a most successful foreign
king, but has just got a new god of his own. If only he could be
convinced that there is but One True God! Isaiah tries. And
this is how he has Yahweh introduce himself to Cyrus: "Thus
sayeth the Lord to his anointed, to Cyrus, whose right hand I
have holden, to subdue nations before him . . . that thou
mayest know that I the Lord, which call thee by thy name, am
the God of Israel. For Jacob my servant's sake, and Israel mine
elect, I have even called thee by thy name: I have surnamed
thee, though thou hast not known me. I am the Lord, and there
is none else, there is no God besides me: I girded thee, though
thou hast not known me" (45:1–5).

This salute to Cyrus is sandwiched between two iconoclastic outbursts, completely off the point in the case of Cyrus, who had an iconoclastic reform movement on at home in Persia, and was anyway far too preoccupied with Lydia, Ionia, and Egypt to pay attention to this part of Isaiah's propositions. But while Assyria, all muscles, had gloried in devastation, the Persians, more sinews and brains, avoided unnecessary destruction. By Persian decree the Jews were free to go back and run their countries as part of a tribute-paying satrapy, thus clearing for Persia the way to Egypt. Some cultural exchange, however, had taken place, and the Prophets brought home eschatology, an organized demonology, the Devil and Hell. Durable articles of faith, still in use.

Apropos Nine

To my astonishment I read in English daily papers in
January, 1960: " 'The Devil and all his works' are dropped
from the revised catechism. . . ." I shall miss him, was my
first reaction. My second: what bad manners! After we have
made him Lucifer, the Prince of Darkness, and, after all,
the Adversary of our Lord, he is given the sack,
"dropped" in a newspaper.

In April the Devil was back, on trial. What had happened
during the intervening months was this: a commission
appointed by the Archbishops of Canterbury and York, taking
note of the changed social conditions, decided the time had
come to modernize Christian teachings and to change the old
phrase: "I would renounce the Devil and all his works,
the pomps and vanity of this wicked world and all the
lusts of the flesh," for a simple: "I would renounce all that is
wrong and fight against evil." Compared with the
glamour of the old sentence, the new one was admittedly
drab and unattractive; and the Church of England
was fighting a losing battle against her congregation's
emotions: "We discovered that there was more deep feeling on
this issue than on any other. Many letters poured in, and
we felt we were bound to leave the Devil in." And the

commission compromised. The words now read,
"I would renounce the Devil and fight evil."

Whereupon, under the headline "Back to the Devil" a
newspaper declared in April: "The Church of England must be
congratulated on having decided to have second thoughts about
the iniquitous proposal to remove the Devil from the
catechism. As a Church dignitary pointed out recently, there is
really no reason why future generations should be misled on
a matter of such practical importance."

P RACTICAL IMPORTANCE is the heart of the matter; for,
"The multitude must be restrained by invisible terrors
and suchlike pageantry. For this reason I think, not that
the ancients acted rashly and at haphazard in introducing
among people notions concerning the gods and beliefs in the
terror of hell, but that moderns are most foolish and rash in
banishing such beliefs." The rash and foolish moderns Polybius
is rapping here are a commission of roughly twenty-two hundred
years ago who thought the time had come to do away with some
of the cruder superstitions (*History* 6.56) .

Men like Plato, Isocrates, Polybius, and Strabo, however,
strongly advocated the continuation of religious superstitions as
a means of control. Strabo put it quite bluntly: "The great mass
of women and common people cannot be induced by mere force
of reason to devote themselves to piety, virtue and honesty;
superstition must therefore be employed, and even this is insuffi-
cient without the aid of the marvellous and the terrible. . . .
For what are . . . all the paraphernalia of antique theology,
but fables employed by founders of states as bugbears to
frighten timorous minds?" (1.8) .

Nevertheless, twenty-two hundred years later we timorous
minds still will not let go of our bugbears. Fear of Hell has been
a tremendously useful social force, and I may be wrong in thinking it rather embarrassing that we still ask to be frightened into
decency by Devil and Hell. With remarkable insight into the
development of human consciousness, Isocrates said: "It is by

the power of persuading one another that we have raised ourselves above the level of the beasts, founded cities, laid down
laws, and discovered arts" (*Antidosis* 254). Accordingly, I wish
the shepherds of the Church of England had tried harder to per-
suade the sheep of their flock to put the Devil and Hell where
we put the Stork and Santa Claus some time ago. But it seems
that hell-fire is like a strong drug: some people are addicted and
take a delight in the torments of religion and in suffering.

Suffering was considered by Buddha as a sore, an affliction,
and he was against it. He did nothing spectacular to relieve the
world of it. After a short indulgence in ascetic deprivation,
which he recognized to be wrong, he taught a do-it-yourself way,
sound and hard self-control, without a saviour and God. Self-
control and compassion is about all that is needed to reduce
suffering. Man is in charge of his own life and has to shoulder
responsibility. That wrongdoing inevitably backfires is the law
of Eastern ethics: it is not a matter of sin and punishment.

The West has chosen a religion with a Father-God who
punishes disobedience, which is sin. His Son chooses the way of
suffering and death, thus giving suffering a new virtue. While
the dying gods of antiquity had suffered, died, and arisen with
crops for the life of Man, Jesus died for mankind the horrible
death that was meant to relieve the world from the horror of
death. Fear of death had been largely removed in a beautiful
and gentle way by Epicurus; but he did not promise the bodily
resurrection of the dead, and the very primitivity of this prospect proved to be irresistible. It appeals to the megalith-builder
in me, and I fully understand the impatience of the many who
predicted Doomsday for tomorrow throughout the last two thousand years.

I fail to see any virtue in suffering *per se*. Whether suffering
leads to a growing awareness or to crime or to
supercilium stoicum or to T. E. Lawrence's Turkish Delight,
is obviously a matter of individual response.

Apropos Ten

THE FIRST STAGES of Yahwism resemble in more than one respect modern rocketry. In both cases "hot stuff" is being handled, with unforeseeable consequences. The effect of rockets is first of all an intentional change of matter, predictable to a limited extent; while the launching of Yahwism caused changes in the human mind, unforeseen and unintended by Moses. In both cases a national issue is involved at the beginning; and in both cases tremendous noise is made before the launching, and then the thing either won't get off or disintegrates untimely. But when the spiritual rocket finally got off, it proved to be a three-stage rocket, all three stages orbiting in our sometimes overcast mind ever since: Yahweh, God, and Allah.

According to the Bible, Yahwism did not get off at all well and was more than once on the brink of disintegration, in spite of the tremendous propulsive energy of prophetic propaganda. The College of Propaganda of the Roman Church wants to convert the rest of the globe, whereas the Prophets as propagandists of Yahweh aimed to turn none but the chosen people into the vehicle of Yahweh. It was a Sisyphean labor and took more or less a thousand years, for the chosen tribes inherited not only the land, but also the gods that went with the land. These gods were called the Baalim by the Prophets.

What sort of a god was Baal? Uniting in his office the functions of diverse departmental gods, he shows monotheistic tendencies. He is the bull-god, signifying the sun, and marrying the moon, Asherah, as a heifer. He is the god of thunder, storm, and rain, like Hadad, Teshub, Zeus, and Indra. He is the dying god like Tammuz, Adonis, Osiris, and Dionysus, and like these also the god of resurrection. As Melkarth he is the city-god of Tyre, and as such takes on not only a Hercules but a Poseidon aspect at Cyprus, Rhodes, Carthage, and Gades. His sister, wife, and widow, known as Anat, Astarte, Tanit, and Asherah, was goddess of war, but "she never ceased to be the goddess of love and fertility, even though in this capacity she was overshadowed by Aleyan-Baal, who became the giver of life par excellence. Therefore, she was his consort with whom he had passionate marital intercourse, described in the manner of the sacred marriage mythology . . ." (E. O. James, *Myth and Ritual in the Ancient Near East*, p. 123).

To us there is a world of difference between Yahweh and Baal. To the Israelites the two were almost indistinguishable, as is obvious from archaeological and biblical evidence. This and the extraordinarily prolonged gestation period of Yahwism had baffled me greatly ever since I became aware of them, until I stumbled over the word Baal itself. Could one of the reasons for the time lag be a linguistic one? Even at the risk of barking up the wrong tree, it seems to me worth pausing to consider whether it could have been the Semitic language that complicated the progress of the new god.

The most embarrassing thing about Baal is his name; and the Christian Fathers would not have hesitated to blame the matter squarely on the Devil, for Baal means Lord with a capital L. This must have led to a tremendous muddle. We must try to imagine that age of universal Polytheism, when the world was "full of gods"—and in Polytheism the word "god," in Hebrew "el," is purely generic and has no more weight than, say, our word "Sir." Now come the Prophets, preaching the glory of a new god whose name is not to be used. This last feature was nothing unusual. Names of gods were often not to be mentioned, taboo, as among the Egyptians, Hittites, and Greeks. Herodotus and Plutarch tie themselves in knots, speaking at length about a god without mentioning his name. What kind of a god is this new god of Moses and the Prophets? Since he is above all other gods, he must be the Lord. What word did the Prophets use for "Lord"? There are two equivalent words in the ancient Semitic language of Palestine, Baal and Adon, both unfortunately the name and title of the two ancient fertility gods of Canaan. Emphatically driving home the point that Yahweh and Yahweh only is the LORD, the Prophets use the word incessantly. And when in the ensuing confusion the tribes of Israel and Judah went a-whoring after Baal and Adonis, it was not altogether "stiff-necked backsliding," but rather due to a large-scale misunderstanding, sprung from synonymous words, that lasted until Greek became the universal language of the ancient Near East.

Even then, it seems, the holy appellations continued to be a stumbling block, if the Fuad fragment proves the case in point. On page 222 of his *Archaeology of Palestine,* Albright writes in a different context about "the Fuad fragment of the Greek Deuteronomy, in which the scribe left blank spaces wherever later Greek texts have *Kyrios,* 'the Lord'; in these spaces a Jewish scribe then inserted the four Aramaic (square Hebrew) letters of the divine name YHWH, which was no longer pronounced, but simply written and replaced in reading by *Adonai,* 'my Lord.'" Josephus hardly uses the word, and in the rare instances where he does, he puts "Despot," which looks odd indeed.

Was it then really the Prophets' predicament to be doomed to misunderstanding by their language? The Semitic languages were extremely rich in metaphor and imagery, but it seems as if there was no image, no epithet left at the new God's arrival that had not been already inherited by some other god, and that Yahweh could not be launched as Lord without being taken for Baal and Adonis. The few attempts to launch him as "King" were quickly abandoned, apparently again for linguistic reasons, for "King" in Semitic languages was Melech, Molech, or Mo-

loch, the appellation of the most abominable of the Baalim, to
whom children were sacrificed, to the horror of the Prophets, the
Christians, and even Sir James Frazer.

> Frazer's reaction came to me as a most unpleasant surprise.
> To avoid any misunderstanding, I quote the
> whole passage: "But amongst the Semites the practice of
> sacrificing their children was not confined to kings.
> In times of great calamity, such as pestilence, drought,
> or defeat in war, the Phoenicians used to sacrifice one of their
> dearest to Baal. 'Phoenician history', says an ancient writer,
> 'is full of such sacrifices.' The writer of a dialogue ascribed to
> Plato observes that the Carthaginians immolated
> human beings as if it were right and lawful to do so, and some
> of them, he adds, even sacrificed their own sons to Baal.
> When Gelo, tyrant of Syracuse, defeated the Carthaginians in
> the great battle of Himera, he required as a condition of
> peace that they should sacrifice their children to Baal no longer.
> But the barbarous custom was too inveterate
> and too agreeable to Semitic modes of thought to be so easily
> eradicated, and the humane stipulation of the
> Greek despot probably remained a dead letter"
> (*The Golden Bough*, Vol. 4, *The Dying God*, p. 167) .

The last sentence reveals a sentiment "too agreeable to
anti-Semitic modes of thought to be easily eradicated," to use
Frazer's own words. Since Jew-baiting anti-Semitism has
become too disreputable and definitely unscientific, it is
replaced by this once-removed anti-Semitism towards
everything Phoenician or Carthaginian. Book reviewers seldom
fail to air these Sunday-school feelings whenever Phoenicia
enters the field. It is the Christian and Classical spirit we were
brought up in: the unquestionable humanity of the Greeks
versus the notorious bestiality of the Phoenician Semites.

In previous paragraphs Frazer had just shown that
child-sacrifice had been a universal practice, also found

among the humane Greeks: indeed, that the Greeks most of the
time did not even bother to sacrifice undesired children,
but just threw them away.

Returning to the Phoenicians, Frazer quotes Philo of Byblos:
"It was ancient custom in a crisis of great danger that
the ruler should give his beloved son for the whole people."
According to him, a Phoenician king sacrificed "his only
begotten son." So did God, according to the New Testament.

But we are still deep in the Old Testament, where the Prophets, in a perpetual harangue, beseech the people to follow "the
Lord," and the harassed people do not and cannot understand
Who is Who. In the eighth century the Prophet Hosea makes a
bold attempt to break free of this linguistic entanglement. "And
it shall be at that day, saith the Lord, that thou shalt call me
Ishi [my husband]; and shalt call me no more Baali [my Lord].
For I will take away the name of the Baalim out of their mouth,
and they shall no more be remembered by their name" (3:16–
17).

The new image worked in an unexpected way, but it did not
eliminate the Baalim or the name. Scholars have generally
agreed that this plural form was used as a convenient lump title
for the fertility gods. But the plural might also have been
stressed to mark the singularity of Yahweh.

Apropos Eleven

THE BOOKS of the Kings give an excellent impression of the interpenetration of Yahweh and Baal worship, and of the incessant fight the Prophets fought against Baalim. There are golden calves and gold-plated images all over, and it is rather obvious that Yahweh and Baal cults are not strictly separated.

But in the contest of prophets at Mount Carmel they are. It is a magnificent story, and should be read (I Kings 17–18). Needless to say, it is a rain-making contest, for Elijah is well aware that only the god who is able to send rain can be Lord of Canaan. Elijah has reason to be highly confident, but only up to a point, and the situation becomes most dramatic and tense.

Ahab, King of Israel, "took to wife Jezebel, the daughter of Ethbaal king of the Zidonians, and went and served Baal, and worshipped him. And he reared up an altar for Baal in the house of Baal, which he had built in Samaria. And Ahab made a grove; and Ahab did more to provoke the Lord God of Israel to anger than all the kings of Israel that were before him" (16:31–3). Whereupon Elijah says to Ahab that there shall be no rain these years, and there is none. Therefore Jezebel has all the prophets of Yahweh slain, and it seems only Elijah is left. Then Elijah, with breath-taking boldness, challenges the entire priesthood of Baal to a rain-making contest on Mount Carmel:

"Then said Elijah unto the people, I remain a prophet of the Lord; but Baal's prophets are four hundred and fifty men. Let them therefore give us two bullocks; and let them choose one bullock for themselves, and cut it in pieces, and lay it on wood, and put no fire under: and I will dress the other bullock, and lay it on wood, and put no fire under: And call ye on the name of your gods, and I will call on the name of the Lord: and the God, that answereth by fire, let him be God. And all the people answered and said, It is well spoken."

The prophets of Baal set to work immediately, while Elijah watches the sacrificial fuss and frills, the leaping and the incessant entreating of Baal to "answer by fire." And nothing happens. "And it came to pass at noon, that Elijah mocked them, and said, Cry aloud: for he is a god; either he is talking, or he is pursuing, or he is in a journey, or peradventure he sleepeth, and must be awaked."

Here he refers to the habits of the gods of Mesopotamia.
When prayers were not answered, the worshiper did
not doubt the god's capacity, but reflected that the god might
have been asleep or on a journey or otherwise busy.
In that case one had better write a letter: and delightful
letters to the gods have been excavated. Thorkild Jacobson has
published one in *Before Philosophy,* and his description
of the functions of the Mesopotamians' "personal god"
is a masterpiece. It is the individual's "personal god"
that is the most important figure in the whole pantheon and to
him the letter is written. He is the indispensable
mediator between the worshiper and the "high gods" who, of
course, cannot be approached by every Tom, Dick, and Harry:
"The personal god is not remote and awesome like
the great gods; he is near and familiar; and he cares." He is
the go-between who has connections with the most high places.
"He moves in the circles of the great gods, knows
them well," writes Jacobson confidently. When in trouble, write
to him. The letter writer is obviously in trouble
and sulking. He feels neglected and does not fail to hint

cunningly that by such neglect the gods lose faithful worshipers, "who are hard to get and difficult to replace." The letter runs:

> To the god my father speak: thus says Apiladad, thy servant:
> 'Why have you neglected me [so]?
> Who is going to give you one who can take my place?
> Write to the god Marduk, who is fond of you,
> that he might break my bondage;
> then I shall see your face and kiss your feet!
> Consider also my family, grown-ups and little ones;
> have mercy on me for their sake, and let your help reach me!'

Whether asleep or on a journey, waking up or returning, the god will find his correspondence, and things will begin to happen.

Baal's priests carry on until evening, and nothing happens. It is getting monotonous, attention is flagging, evening is falling; and this is the moment Elijah has been waiting for. Baal has not answered. Now he will call on his God, who is the Lord. And he asks the multitude to draw closer and watch his doings. He builds an altar of rough stones with a trench around it, cuts up the bullock, and places the pieces on wood with no fire underneath. Meanwhile the time of the evening sacrifice has come, and it is getting dark. But instead of invoking his God, Elijah has four barrels of water poured over the sacrifice: three times this procedure is repeated, until everything is thoroughly drenched and the trench is filled. And now Elijah raises his voice: "Lord God of Abraham, Isaac, and of Israel, let it be known this day that thou art God. . . . Then the fire of the Lord fell and consumed the burnt sacrifice, and the wood, and the stones, and the dust, and licked up the water that was in the trench. And when all the people saw it, they fell on their faces; and they said, The Lord, he is the God! the Lord, he is the God!" (18:37–9).

This would be enough to convert every unbeliever, and is a spectacle after my own heart. But still, where is the rain? Elijah's "There is a sound of abundance of rain" did not ease my apprehension as I read. But Elijah proceeds with outward calm. He has the prophets of Baal slain, and sends Ahab to partake in the sacrificial meal. "And he went up to the top of Carmel, and cast himself down upon the earth, and put his face between his knees. And he said to his servant, Go up now, look toward the sea. And he went up, and looked, and said, There is nothing." Six times he went and there was nothing. At last the seventh time: "Behold, there ariseth a little cloud out of the sea. And Elijah said, Go up, say unto Ahab, Prepare thy chariot, and get thee down, that the rain stop thee not. And it came to pass in the mean while, that the heaven was black with clouds and wind, and there was a great rain. And Ahab rode. . . ." And Elijah, mad with joy, girded up his loins and raced ahead of the king's chariot. And this is simply glorious: he does not get pompous, but mad with joy. It is very likely this beautiful story that provoked Jeremiah's exclamation: "Are there any among the vanities of the Gentiles that can cause rain?"

Elijah's showmanship is magnificent, second only to that of Moses. But all theater and show business, of course, had its origin in religious spectacles, long before Dionysus whose cult gave birth to Greek theater. "It is at the outset one and the same impulse that sends a man to church and to the theatre," says Jane E. Harrison in *Ancient Art and Ritual* (pp. 9–10). Archaeology has unearthed numerous "libretti," texts spoken at spectacles performed in the temples of the ancient Near East. Ancient religion was show business. One of the cardinal tasks of ancient priesthoods was to provide entertainment meant to please both the gods and the multitude. The Roman Church fully grasped the importance of entertainment, though it was finally outdone by the Inquisition, who did not hesitate to revive human sacrifices as public entertainment, with "heretics" as burnt offerings. In the Old Testament the slaying of heretics, namely the priesthood of Baal, is done off stage. Under Elijah's conduct an enormous tension is built up towards the climax, the consumption of the burnt offering by "the fire of the Lord." He or Elisha also knew how to keep the naturally irreverent

exuberance of children down; and the story in II Kings (2:23–
4) is obviously meant to impress children in fairy-tale fashion:
"And he went up from thence unto Bethel: and as he was going
up by the way, there came forth little children out of the city,
and mocked him, and said unto him, Go up, thou bald head; go
up, thou bald head. And he turned back, and looked on them,
and cursed them in the name of the Lord. And there came forth
two she-bears out of the wood, and tare forty and two children
of them."

When I later read in the second book of the Maccabees that
the water Elijah poured on the sacrifice was naphtha,
I felt as I always feel when my friend John, who is an
enchanting conjurer, tells me how it is done. I am
much happier with perfect magic than with perfect know-how.

To us, who are familiar with infrared heat and ultraviolet
light, naphtha is old-fashioned and vulgar stuff;
but at the time of the Prophets it was a mysterious substance,
apparently not known to the Phoenicians. To Alexander
in Babylon it seemed fabulous. Not believing that the
water-clear liquid could burn, he poured it over a boy and
lit him. To his astonishment the boy burned. Plutarch,
who tells the story, presumes rightly that naphtha must have
been used a lot in magic. Roughly a thousand
years after Elijah it was most effectively employed as the
basic substance in flame throwers, called "Greek Fire,"
at the defense of Constantinople against the Arabs.
This Greek Fire was also styled God-sent, a
supernatural agent, revealed to the Emperor Constantine by
angels as a special favor to the Romans, who
were then the chosen people.

Apropos Twelve

I T WAS another thousand years before we discovered, among other properties, the propulsive power of the "fire of the Lord" and harnessed it. Aren't we rather slow?

> You glorify nature and meditate on her,
> Why not domesticate her and regulate her?
> You obey nature and sing her praise,
> Why not control her course and use it?

That was written around 300 B.C. by Hsün-Tze (quoted from Hu-Shih, *Development of the Logical Method in Ancient China,* p. 152). What on earth were we doing all the time? We produced some remarkable art, though most of the time we went to the wars as usual. But although wars, we are told, accelerate Man's creativity and ingenuity, it looks as if, apart from art, we had spent almost two thousand years mainly on metaphysics, on theological and philosophical speculations. The paralyzing twin superstitions of Greek and Christian thinking, Hybris and Sin, proved powerful enough to prevent Western Man from employing his mind as a useful tool for utilitarian purposes, and Prometheus remained bound until the last century.

Like all primitives, I prefer spectacles to speculations, and a good show gives me an intense pleasure. Therefore I greatly admire the stagecraft of the Roman Church, and I shall never forget an Easter Saturday Mass in a Dominican monastery in Canada. I went at the request of the late Père Couturier, who knew my weakness, and it was a truly great experience: a magnificent, a superbly conducted and executed religious performance, aesthetically a marvel, tense with magic. In spite of my ignorance of the intrinsic doctrine, I immensely enjoyed the ceremony. In his book *The Hero with a Thousand Faces,* Joseph Campbell gives an excellent interpretation of the ritual as a variant of the Sacred Marriage (p. 250).

Interpretations of strange rituals can have their pitfalls, even for the most benevolent onlooker. Ibn-Shuad, a historian and poet of Moorish Spain, was a fond admirer of Christian ritual. Watching the administration of the sacrament at midnight mass in Cordova, he was enchanted by the candles, the bells, the wreathing incense, the costumes of the priests and the altar boys, and his moving account runs thus: "How often in that church have I breathed the scent of the wine of youth, enhanced with the bouquet of old age from the priest. . . . Young lads toasted me with wine, blushing with modesty like the tender gazelle under the eye of his lord. . . . They took communion with him, these delicate lads, and he gave them wine and pork to eat" (Edwin Hole, *Andalus,* p. 142). He certainly was misled by his enthusiasm, this charming Muslim, but I do not for a moment doubt that in his transport of joy over a misunderstood ritual of the infidels, he was nearer to God than the Inquisition in her zealous extermination of infidels.

Speaking of the stagecraft of the Roman Church, which I enjoy, I do infinitely exclude the spectacles of the Inquisition, staged during the centuries of the Church's relapse into her lowest barbarity, when she became very Roman indeed. What the Circus had been to the Romans, the Inquisition became to the Church—her Circus Maximus with pomp and circumstance. For lack of lions and other wild beasts, the victims were thrown to human beasts, superior to lions in beastly inventiveness, for the glory of God. As for the Protestants, it was the spectacles they disapproved of, not all the torture and burning, and this cannot be swept under the altar. According to Calvin, heresy is worse than murder, and he was all for burning. A Persian Sufi, an infidel, was of different opinion: "All religions are interpretations of the same dream." The wisdom and *noblesse* of this saying are unsurpassed, and I wish the next international Church Council would choose it as a slogan, would meet at Jerusalem, and would agree to give up their absurd religious pecking order in a pantheon full of Only True Gods.

While not wanting to hurt anybody's Bronze Age feelings, I think it might ameliorate human relations if we tried to comprehend the origin and nature of our religious claims, whether territorial ones based on Bronze Age pledges, or our Christian claims of licensed superiority, based on posthumous records of Jesus' disciples and the interpretation of Paul.

Thinking of the interpretations of Marx's and Freud's disciples, likewise filled with apostolic and Pauline zeal, one is bound to wonder how the teachings of Jesus actually looked. Which is a futile reflection. But still, I think it worth while to investigate how far our claims are aetiological rationalizations to justify material, emotional, or spiritual needs and greeds. Unless we prefer the time-honored ostrich-policy that makes us feel so definitely better than thou, which we never could do with open eyes. The ostrich-position has advantages: that way we can never lose face. And, let us not forget, the ostrich-position is legitimate fun for the onlooker. Which brings me back to spectacles.

There was the beatification of a Spaniard in St. Peter's, that formidable Grand Central Station of Christendom where everything is bigger and better than life. It was a stupendous mass-affair, a real crossbreed between a Solemn High Mass and a football game, that could only be described in journalese. When Pope Pius XII was carried in, looking gloriously decorative and handsome in his papal splendor, raising beautiful hands in beautiful benedictions, the crowd went into a frenzy, waving hats, sticks, scarves, and handkerchiefs, shouting "Papa, Papa," and I felt carried away and happy and not a bit out of place.

There was also Ignatius Loyola's visit to Palma de Mallorca. To be more precise, it was his skull, or rather a piece of his skull, a relic, that came for a week. In spite of my passion for all things pagan I almost missed it, and just caught the end. Flags, tapestries, and draperies were out, and I was told: "The skull is leaving the island today." But nobody knew where and nobody cared. I did, and was determined to see the skull off. But where? There came marines, in gala, marching towards the harbor, and I followed them hopefully until I found myself faced by three battleships, in full regalia, and all the marines lined up motionless. And nothing happened, as if Elijah were conducting and building up suspense. At last, distant cannon blasts. I did not count them, but an Englishman next to me did. "That is more than the Queen gets," he said with slight disapproval. Finally a cavalcade appeared in black, with white feathers in their bonnets, and after them an authentic eighteenth-century golden coach with numerous coach- and footmen in eighteenth-century costumes, and behind them, equally splendid, a wave of high clergy who took the relic out of the golden coach and carried it solemnly onto a battleship. Which thereupon exploded. At least, that was what I thought when it started firing left and right and up and down. And I rejoiced and was all for Spain again: is there another country in the world that would use battleships to carry a holy bone from one place to another?

But this is fetishism, I hear someone mutter. Of course it is fetishism, beautiful fetishism. And the money it costs! Good spectacles cost money and are worth it. While rocketry is not. Rocketry is a paradigm case of "conspicuous waste." Twelfth-century France, in a holy rapture aiming heavenwards, spent one million dollars on cathedrals in honor of the Queen of Heaven, and was broke for centuries to come. But the cathedrals are still there, and among them is Chartres. Whereas rockets . . .

Apropos Thirteen

To BAN THE BOMB will be just as difficult as to ban the stocks and stones, the ancient phallic symbols of fertility and life. But it was not only the symbols that infuriated Moses and the Prophets: a truly Victorian fuss is raised to conceal "the shameful thing" itself. It starts with the fig leaves in Eden. Furthermore, the altars shall have no steps, for on steps the priests' nakedness might be visible. To play safe, the priests are put into linen breeches that go from here to there.

This still goes on: pants for the natives are still of great concern to the missionary. According to Strabo and others, the Phoenicians introduced clothes to the hitherto naked natives of the Balearic Islands, called Gymnasiae for that reason. But they certainly did not encourage the naked to deck themselves with clothes for puritanical reasons. As good businessmen, they "created a demand" for textiles, and then supplied the new market. Not without erecting a few pillars, which are still there.

As for the pillars: I wonder if everything had a proper look at the Eucharistic Congress in Bombay, for the Indians are rather careless in these matters. From time immemorial they have had "the shameful thing" on altars or as altars, in temples or as temples, for to them it is the image and

symbol of life, and venerable. As Gandhi wrote in a letter,
it had never occurred to him that there was any obscene
significance to it until Christian missionaries told him.

For this reason, the Bomb could never have originated in
India. But Western Man, obeying the biblical code,
had for two thousand years dutifully repressed a great part of
his libidinous strivings, dutifully sublimating them
into more and more abstract ideas, formulas and figures that
produced in the end, as the crowning achievement of his
sublimation, something that has taken the exact shape of the
shameful thing and explodes in ejaculations of a
magnitude and ostentation that must dazzle everybody and be
reward enough for all frustration. To ban the Bomb
would mean nothing less than to castrate Man's Potency
Regained. Regained after and through the agony of
millennial sublimation. Therefore, although we disapproved,
we now can understand de Gaulle, who, doubly frustrated
as a Christian and a war-general, could not resist the
temptation in the desert.

One look at any nuclear-power engine is convincing:
there is no imagery left, no evanescent anthropomorphism.
It leaves us cold. Whereas the bombs and rockets
are a joy to behold, whether on launching pads, the high
places of the Atom age, or on triumphal floats in parades,
putting to shame the humble stocks and stones that were
paraded in the same manner at fertility rites of old, as can be
seen on Greek vases. The trouble is that today's
ejaculations are anything but fertile.

If there is such a thing as Hybris and Sin in the world, this
is it. While more than half of the Human Race is
suffering hunger and want, the two big powers have
started wasting billions and billions in a Space Race for
Prestige. As if it were just a little boys' piddling contest,
which it resembles in more than one respect. I wish Freud had

lived long enough to witness this incredible spectacle.
He believed ultimately in reason, and therefore
disclosed to us the devastating powers of un-reason that
govern us. But never could he have dreamed up such a gigantic
display of classical Freudian un-reason. "Freedom from Prestige"
is now one of our most urgent needs.

The Bomb I reject even as a vehicle of transport into the
Other World, as too expensive and against all the rules
of the A.S.P.C.A. Furthermore, I am prejudiced, not against the
Other World as the inner world, but against the
Other World as the Hereafter, which is just one department of
the inner world. None of the Other World posters
and prospects, Western or Eastern, has sufficient attraction to
evoke my nostalgia. None of them can compare with this world.
And towards this world and this transitory life
I have turned my full curiosity.

There is a realm in the human mind where we find freedom,
and where we retreat whenever we tire, despair, or fail to cope
with the manifold obstacles of this world: the inner world. This
realm is indispensable for recreation and creation. Here is Eden,
here is Heaven (and Hell), here is Paradise, Nirvana, and
Alcheringa. Here is Utopia, here is everybody from Plato in
Wonderland to Walter Mitty, from highly organized metaphysical structures to everybody's daydreams. And as citizens of both
worlds, inner and outer, our mental balance and sanity seem to
depend on an equilibrium of this double citizenship.

From the middle of the last millennium B.C., Man took a
noticeable turn towards the Other World, in some cases with a
vehemence that upset the mental balance deeply; and the dis-
turbed psychometabolism caused conspicuous symptoms of a
toxic, a delirious state of mind, a hallucinatory frenzy, a holy
delirium tremens, palpable in many of the Greek, Gnostic, and
Christian metaphysical systems.

The Chinese were only slightly affected. When around 450
B.C. Mo Ti started preaching universal love, disarmament, and

peace on earth, he was nearly killed for it, and silenced by sober Confucianism. The Indians ceased to take this world seriously. It became Maya and did not matter any longer. But they never made the mistake of not enjoying it.

In Greece, Plato declared this world to be rotten, which, after the Peloponnesian War, the bankruptcy of Athens, and Socrates' death, indeed it was. He turned his back on the world in aristocratic disgust and retired into the realm of metaphysics, where he moved only among Ideas and found security in thinking in perfect circles. Here he wrote his *Republic,* a planned nightmare and totalitarian's Bible. But Plato's dreams of superman will never fail to appeal to the adolescent mind.

The Jews had not fared well in this world. Nor, for that matter, had any other of the Near Eastern nations. The utter discouragement and frustration froze part of the Jews in their tracks, while others followed the trend of the time to blame this world and flung themselves vehemently into the comforting and compensating doctrines of the Other World. The Levant, ravaged by incessant conquests and wars, was under duress and in a delirious apocalyptic mood, and the Revelation was only one of many similar documents. More than ever the countries were infested with prophets, sibyls, oracles, orgies, mysteries, daemons, devils, spirits, angels, portents, and omens. Everything was foretelling and miracles, and everybody was ready to believe everything and did so.

Even the Jews at last believed in Yahweh. And Jesus believed Yahweh to be his Father, who expected this "only-begotten Son" to sacrifice himself for the good of mankind, and thus to show his believers the way into the Other World, the Kingdom of Heaven. After due provocation of the Establishment his death wish was fulfilled, and he was tried, sentenced, and executed by the Romans. Consequently his death was blamed on the Jews, a superstition still cherished by Christians, whose ignorance has wilfully been nourished by their theologians. Insisting on the privileges of his God-Sonship, Jesus had ingrained into his disciples the belief that admission into the heavenly kingdom could be granted exclusively through himself. To believe in God was no longer enough, although he had stated, "I and the Father are One." "Now is the Son of Man glorified, and God is glorified in him. If God be glorified in him, God shall also glorify him in himself, and shall straightway glorify him," as John explained it admirably in his gospel (13:31-2). Writing in Ephesus, John also equated Jesus with the Logos, a discovery of Heraclitus, another Ephesian. And Paul believed that Jesus' death had liberated mankind from the terror of death forever, and exclaimed triumphantly: "O Death, where is thy sting?" The additional sting is in condemnation and Hell, as if death had not been bad enough as it was.

The New Testament, we are taught, teaches us to die for a cause. The Old Testament, I found, teaches us to live for a cause, to cleave to a cause in spite of everything. I am on the side of life, and wish some Jew would teach us at last how to inhabit this planet properly instead of aiming at the moon. But why a Jew? Because for a convincingly long time we have given obvious preference to Jewish ideologies, including anti-Semitism.

Apropos Fourteen

As BEFITS an age of semi-ignorance, anti-Semitism has been one of our foremost superstitions for more than two thousand years. Although I am, of course, superstitious, I have never indulged in this one. Rather, I indulged in philo-Semitic crusading, which made me feel good, as all crusading does. It always benefits the crusader most.

To get to the root of anti-Semitism, one must begin at the beginning of Semitism. To summarize as briefly as possible: Moses felt called by a new god to establish a strictly exclusive theocracy in a more or less clearly defined Near Eastern territory. The new god committed himself repeatedly, to a selected group of Semitic tribes, to the effect that he would give them the promised land as an inheritance forever. Due to unfavorable circumstances in the ancient Near East, this promise could not be fulfilled. Man wants to know reasons, and, as Frankfort said, the primitive mind does not look "for the *how,* but for the *who,* when it looks for a cause" (*Before Philosophy,* p. 24).

Who is to blame? Even in Polytheism gods are not often blamed, because to whitewash gods and to blacken Man is the *raison d'être* of all theology. To justify the god's way to Man is the theologian's irrational business.

In the Prophets' case, who is to be blamed for the national disaster but the Jews? Furthermore, not only the political but

any misfortune at all has to be blamed on the new god's worshipers, who happen to be Jews. Thus the Old Testament becomes the first and most eloquent anti-Semite document in
history. In principle the Prophets do not differ from other
theologians: to exalt God, Man must be put in the wrong.
Sometimes Man talks back. The Hittite King Mursilis complains
angrily: "What is this, O gods, that you have done! You have let
in a plague, and the land of Hatti, all of it is dying, so no one
prepares the offerings of food and drink [for you]. And you
come to us, O gods, and for this matter you hold us guilty . . ."
(Gurney, *The Hittites*, p. 157).

"And for this matter you hold us guilty." If they once ceased
to make their believers feel guilty, theologians could fold up. To
get the right grip on the believer it is essential to smash his self-
confidence, to evoke and manipulate a bad conscience. Like
ambitious politicians, the Prophets never put the well-being of
the people before their own ambitious theological aims. "To
magnify God" is their sole aim, and they feel justified in load-
ing every mishap onto the shoulders of the Jews, drowning every
possible argument in torrents of inexhaustible Jew-baiting.
Those relentless and noisy accusations of the new god's people,
the Jews, could not remain unheard in a country that was an
open thoroughfare, where the Prophets "stood in the gate"
pouring forth their abusive anti-Semitic scorn. I cannot help seeing these things in as primitive terms as they probably deserve.
The Old Testament's noisy loud-speakers were just as effective
as today's commercials, as our admen know so well: *semper
aliquid haeret,* something always sticks. And it stuck with the
Egyptians, Syrians, Greeks, and Romans, aggravated of course
by common "spheres of interest," commercial rivalry. At the
time of Jesus anti-Semitism was nothing new, as Josephus'
Contra Apionem sufficiently proves.

But while this discrediting of Jews *ad majorem Dei gloriam*
had been a purely domestic affair of Israelite theology, it was
taken over eagerly by Christian theology as soon as the young
Church felt it opportune to sever its Jewish ties, and deliberately and ruthlessly used as a weapon against the Jewish race.

To magnify God, however, is the end of theology, and the end sanctifies the means, including the pious lie that the Jews crucified Jesus. I wonder if our schools could not rectify this piece of ignorance in ancient history. Aware of the old accusations, Jesus said: "Do not think I will accuse you to the Father: there is one that accuseth you, Moses, in whom you trust" (John 5:45). Moses and the Prophets.

As a Jewish ideology, Christianity has inherited the Jews' God, a great part of their scriptures, a ready-made anti-Semitism, and a scapegoat that is always at hand: the Jews living in the midst of Christendom. Thus, having behind it all the powers of unreason from the beginning and fortified by ignorance, anti-Semitism could not fail to get the firm grip it has on the Gentile mind.

If anti-Semites would ever think at all, they might quickly stop aping the Jews in their anti-Semitism. And if the Jews would put their admirable everyday maxim "There are always two possibilities" into practice, or rather into theory, they might give up their archaic Apartheid, which has forced a Monorail style of thinking upon all their ideologies.

Apropos Fifteen

I F I SHOW a certain lack of reverence, or rather of fear of God, it is probably due to childhood experiences, the usual takeoff point for later attitudes. I never received any proper religious instructions in early childhood. Come to think of it, I did not see the inside of a church until my confirmation. From my Lutheran parents I never heard a word for or against any religion. Not that they were irreligious: it was simply that other things apparently mattered more to them. My father taught me to be a good shot, to find the cardinal points in the midst of the woods, and to observe the stars. The servants and peasants talked sometimes about God, but they also talked about Perun, Perkunus, and Potrimpus, the Slavonic gods, and all their superstitions, and I believed everything. They took me tobogganing by moonlight on Potrimpus' hill and gave me a swing on the great ceremonial swing under the oaks, too heavy for children and not meant for them. The moonlight tobogganing carried on at school. One evening my toboggan overturned and, lying on my back in the snow, I saw a heavenly marvel: Halley's comet. And for the first time in my life the end of the world was at hand.

The Lutheran minister, who had baptized me and seemed to prefer our forest to his church, hardly ever talked at all when he came to our house, but went straight to the piano and played

Bach, Beethoven, and Brahms for hours on end. And so, all I could find out about God by myself was this: he seemed to belong to us as important distant relatives do. Only occasionally mentioned, he lived too far away, I gathered, for visitations, like Grandfather. Father, God, and Grandfather were apparently of the same and not altogether harmless species, never fully trusted, and I often wished all three of them would live far away and leave me alone with Mother, who was wing and warmth.

God knew everything, like Father, which was simply awful; and he seemed to be an unpredictable eccentric, like Grandfather, who shot in anger. Not that my grandfather ever dragged his daughters by the hair, as Aksakov's had done: he shot at them with a rifle. It was his way of showing disapproval. He was quick-tempered and shot a lot. As far as I know he never killed anybody, and it was not until his ninety-fourth year that he was shot.

Father, Grandfather, and God were a Trinity with an unmistakable family resemblance, and the only Trinity that ever made sense to me. It was not awe I felt towards them, it was uneasiness and fear. Father was so tall, and roared like a lion. Though he never roared at me, I heard his roar over the house and over the fields, and it struck terror into me. Only much later I learned the meaning of it.

In his reminiscences, Jakob von Uexküll describes a similar childhood experience. "Why is Father so terribly angry?" he asked his mother, hearing his father coming down on one of his men like a thunderstorm. "He is not a bit angry," said his mother. "It is just because these people respect only an angry lord."

This is a lordly and feudal fallacy, a Bronze Age fallacy, an anachronism that hardly works any longer outside the parade ground. A leonine roar frightens children and dogs, but otherwise mostly impresses the lordly roarer's self-esteem: the roared-at men and women shrugged, giggled, and laughed the moment my father's back was turned.

Father also inflicted punishment. Today I am convinced that I deserved all the spankings, and all of them are forgotten but one. That Father had an extremely acute sense of justice I learned later, but once he made a mistake. A double mistake: I was not guilty, and the punishment was not spontaneous but calculated. Rarely have I been so outraged in all my life as then at the age of five or six. All my accumulated indignation broke loose, my rage overrode all fear, and I took the law into my own hands: I marched into my father's bedroom, where he enjoyed the prerogative of the master of the house, staying in bed until ten o'clock after he had driven everybody else out of bed at dawn with the familiar roar. In I marched, clutching the ruler he used to spank me with, and I hit him.

The worm had turned. But my rage was not yet spent. Running out of the house I came across a peasant boy, who, I thought, had not taken his cap off to me fast enough, and I came down on the wretched boy. This became a ritual, and I started a reign of terror of my own, until something unheard-of happened: the boy-worm turned and told his father, who complained to my father, who summoned me and promised me the worst thrashing there was, if I ever touched the boy again. The next time I touched him, not seeing my father behind the shrubs, I did not waste time or words: "And if my father beats me to death—you are going to get your thrashing." And he got it.

This had an unexpected and one-sided result: my father never spanked me again. Which was a state of affairs I could not foresee, for the thunder continued and I kept on expecting the bolt that never struck again. "My daughter had defeated me," my father said later with a broad smile, in truly talmudic fashion. But I did not know it yet.

I had to leave home for school at the age of eight, the First World War came and went, I married young, and when at last I was getting to know my father and see him through grown-up eyes, I had outgrown fear. The thundercloud that overshadowed my infancy had gone. He was still tall and aloof, but the thunder had ceased and I found him very quiet and polite. And in an upsurge of compassion I discovered the humaneness and unspeakable loneliness behind the Victorian thunder-god mask. How was it possible that he had frightened me?

Meanwhile I had met "denominations" and "movements." All of them promised me an introduction to God. He had to be approached by metaphysics, I was told. And, aided by a long febrile illness, I had quite a fling at the high trapeze, and deeply enjoyed moments of blissful vertigo over the abyss. There is a time for everything in life. There also came a time of surrender, when I experienced the euphoria of conversion and the comfort of faith and prayer. It did not last, and after many a-whorings I gave up stalking God. Comparing his tracks with those of other gods, and finding them altogether man-made, I turned to new hunting grounds and went a-whoring for good. With the rest of my metaphysical baggage I lost not only the dreadful jargons acquired along the road but also the sense of sin and guilt, and this was good riddance indeed. Today, in my seventies, I find myself wholeheartedly pedestrian, and, to my astonishment, stalking God again.

Being without any academic qualifications, belonging to no particular group, and trying to build up my own prejudices, I just wonder in my unacademic way how this particular God happened to the mind of Man, as a historical event seen within the Near Eastern context, "that realm of budding bibles." I do not doubt the existence of God, as I do not doubt the existence of Mind and Life: they are three states of affairs we know next to nothing about. Life, according to the Oxford Dictionary, is "a state of ceaseless change and functional activity peculiar to organized matter, and especially to the portion of it constituting an animal or plant before death. . . ." Whatever life is, it seems that in the course of human evolution we have theriomorphized, anthropomorphized, and deified these inexplicable forces, in female and male forms, in Poly- and Monotheism. And all these interpretations are justifiable as expressions of different degrees of awareness. Thus I cannot deny the existence of gods and God as human rationalizations of the deified life process that have a legitimate place in the human mind. And thus every civilization has the gods or God it deserves, as every country has the government it deserves.

Apropos Sixteen

Having another look at this God of ours, we notice that, in contrast to the East, we have not only chosen to believe that we are created by God, but—according to Kierkegaard—even find it "an edifying contemplation that towards God we are always in the wrong." This is not only a medieval but a Bronze Age hair shirt, and with his sense of humor Kierkegaard tried desperately to shed it.
"Everybody is too serious for me," he cried, because "at heart the religious man is humorous."
Unfortunately, his *Angst* was greater than his humor, which often sounds like whistling in the dark.

WHAT ARE OUR glorious Bronze Age heroes, if not successful ruffians, succeeding in most cases by brutal force? The heroic age is a brutal, unwashed barbarian splendor, seen through the romanticizing haze of poetry.
Christian writers, who in anger and embarrassment reject the God of the Old Testament, are at least a humorous sight to the onlooker when they are so obviously embarrassed to find a divine ruffian at the bottom of their ideological pedigree. No matter how noble the family tree, at the bottom is always a common ruffian.

Yahweh is a most uncommon ruffian. He is the paragon of self-made gods, with a career of unparalleled brilliance. With Moses as his champion he created himself, and, under two aliases, reached finally a goal he had not been aiming at as a young god. Man he created in his own image, which is that of a splendid Bronze Age barbarian.

What else could he have been in the Near Eastern Bronze Age, when Man had just entered what Veblen called "the predatory phase of culture," a time when violence, aggression, devastation and slaughter became "honorific employment," glorified in wall paintings and reliefs or in verbal monuments like the Old Testament and the Iliad? Going to the wars and spreading terror was the *sine qua non,* the prime status symbol of the Bronze Age ruler, hero, or god. Thus Yahweh as a Bronze Age god had to go to the wars and "destroy utterly," because these people respected only an angry Lord. Therefore he displays the naïve brutality of a still honestly brutal age and is at his worst under the prophetship of Samuel, who takes a dim view of kingship and has a way with Saul that reminds me of the way my father had with a dog he was breaking in for blind obedience. Allegedly at Yahweh's request, Samuel is breaking Saul and my heart goes out to Saul, while theologians are all for Samuel.

> Bronze is functionally outmoded today and modes of warfare
> have changed, but it does not look as if our frame
> of mind has changed. We have not outgrown or overthrown
> bellicose and predatory attitudes considered "honorific"
> in the Bronze Age. Going to the wars is still a status symbol,
> a distinction, to Primitives among us—and to the
> primitive within us. Having been to the wars was glorified
> by Egyptians, Assyrians, and Greeks in stone
> or otherwise. We glorify the accomplishment in stone,
> on paper, and on celluloid *ad nauseam.* Having been to the
> wars is not enough, however; it must be endlessly written and
> rewritten about, and there is no end to re-enacting
> glorious scenes of slaughter and the minutest display of

brutality on the screen. And then we look down our nose at Yahweh's martial activities.

⌐Had Yahweh emerged in the Bronze Age as the all-transcending god, he would have failed as he had failed in Egypt as Aton; and Moses knew it⌐ From history, it seems that "to destroy utterly" is an almost obligatory stage on the road to civilization, a *rite de passage* of young nations, a transitory phase of uninhibited juvenile delinquency, glorified by bards and prophets as "heroic.'⌐Consequently, forced to accommodate himself to his historical context, Yahweh emerges during the Bronze Age constrained to prove his supremacy by the supreme virtue of the time: martial force. He starts his career with wholehearted enthusiasm, as Lord of Hosts with slaughter and rape.⌐ "For every man a damsel or two," sings Deborah.

Accepting the fact that the epiphany of this god did not take place in a vacuum, but in history, and a rather unrefined stage of history at that, I find myself singing an Apology of Yahweh as a war-god in the face of those refined Christians who object to the un-divine ways Yahweh had in his early career.

But at all stages of his career his way of keeping accounts is truly and traditionally divine. As long as the going is good, he takes all the credit; as soon as the wind changes, the people get all the blame. Success is entered on his side only, failure on theirs only. This is a way of reckoning that only God could get away with. Homer's moral bookkeeping is the opposite: whatever the vicissitudes of the Trojan War, they are almost entirely the doing of the gods, and Man cannot be blamed. In the Old Testament, Man is given responsibility—only too much of it.

Apropos Seventeen

W HY DO the Prophets prefer to express Yahweh's relationship to his people from the eighth century on in terms of matrimony? Other images are employed too, but an obvious preference is given to conjugal terms.

Verbal imagery only is allowed by Moses, and I wonder what caused the prohibition of image-making in other media. Could it be that Moses, who knew Egyptian art, found the chosen people wanting in talent? This thought inevitably occurred to me while I was contemplating the art of the Phoenicians, who indefatigably produced artifacts for over a thousand years without ever losing their delightful mediocrity. Sidney Smith defined Phoenician art as "the composite style which began to be developed in the eighteenth century B.C. and continually absorbed new themes from other arts, without any striking change in style, till the fifth century" (Frankfort, *Art and Architecture of the Ancient Orient,* p. 189) . They never achieved a style of their own, but their touch is unmistakable. The themes are derived from the art of Egypt and Mesopotamia, but in Phoenician hands they lose the rather monotonous magnificence of the originals altogether. Other peoples' religious symbols become "space-fillers," or hybrid creations of only ornamental significance.

The variations on the most solemn Egyptian and
Mesopotamian themes can be hilarious and delightful, and
sometimes the design and craftsmanship
are also superb, as for instance in almost every ivory from
Arslan Tash and Nimrud. And the two bronze
bowls from Nimrud, the animal-chaos and the bird's-eye
mountainscape, are unsurpassed in originality and boldness
of conception.

Still, it was not great art, though it was immensely popular,
as finds from all over the Mediterranean show.
King Solomon and King Ahab were great customers.
But homemade artifacts from Israelite Palestine hardly differ
from ordinary Phoenician or Canaanite products,
which means they are far from what one would expect the
Chosen People's art to be. And officially the image-making of
Israel was restricted to the medium of language.

Yahweh has chosen the heart of the children of Israel as his
local habitation. But it is up to the Prophets to find the clue,
the "name" that opens those hearts, an appellation, an image
that strikes home. As the Holy One, the Creator of Israel, the
Redeemer, the Saviour, the Maker, he is too airy a something to
evoke any response. None of these appellations has any meaning
to the congregation, for none of them conveys any known experience of real life. "The Lord is our judge, the Lord is our
lawgiver. . . ." To establish a transference to a judge or a
lawgiver must be even harder than to establish a transference to
a tax collector.

"King" is rarely used, for reasons already mentioned. The
term "Father" has to be applied with caution in Monotheism,
for it presupposes a mother. Everything that has any resemblance to the surrounding Polytheism must be avoided, and
there is still a long way to go before Jesus can choose this God as
his Father and exalt him to the metaphysical universal father
image of Christianity.

Every kind of possible and impossible imagery is used by the

Prophets to tie these people to this God. "Mine anger was kindled against the shepherds, and I punished the goats: for the Lord of hosts hath visited his flock the house of Judah, and hath made them as his goodly horse in battle." (In this sentence the house of Judah undergoes the astonishing metamorphosis from a flock of goats to God's battle-horse.) "In that day, saith the Lord, I will smite every horse with astonishment" (Zechariah 10:3, 12:4).

Fully aware of the fierce rivalry of prophets and gods, "namely, of the gods of the people which are round about you, nigh unto thee, or far off from thee, from the one end of the earth even unto the other end of the earth," the Deuteronomist, who is a pious lawgiver but a deplorable psychologist, gives a warning: "Take heed to thyself that thou be not snared by following them, . . . and that thou enquire not after their gods, saying, How did these nations serve their gods?" (13:7, 12:30). Did he really expect the children of Israel and Judah not to inquire after this warning? In spite of the prophetic trumpetings of doom and gloom, and all the discouraging dithyrambs of defeatism, they did serve other gods, and at times Yahweh seems almost forgotten.

Conscious or not—as if with acute psychological awareness that without worshipers no god can survive—Hosea equates his conjugal difficulties with his prophetic ones, and expresses Yahweh's relationship with his people in terms of matrimony, or marriage. And he strikes home. For no other image is charged with emotions of such force, or has this emotional grip. Based on physical experience familiar to almost everyone, it remains the image of our most intense strivings for emotional and spiritual union: we embrace a cause, espouse a cause, are wedded to a cause, and cleave to a cause. "How, then," asked Augustine centuries later, "could it be described in such a way that even dull minds could grasp it, except by means of some familiar word?" (*Confessions* 11.4).

In spite of their violent opposition to the ritual of the sacred marriage practiced all around them, neither Jewish nor Christian theologians can do without the image. The Apostle Paul applies wholeheartedly the full-blown marriage imagery in his second letter to the Corinthians: "For I am jealous over you with godly jealousy: for I have espoused you to one husband, that I may present you as a chaste virgin to Christ" (11:2). Augustine employs it frequently, stressing the metaphor—whose anthropomorphism can hardly be called evanescent—to the utmost: "Like a bridegroom Christ went forth from his chamber, he went out with a presage of his nuptials into the field of the world. He came to the marriage bed of the cross, and there, mounting it, he consummated his marriage. And when he perceived the sigh of the creature, he lovingly gave himself up in place of his bride, and he joined himself to the woman forever" (*Sermo Suppositus* 120).

But as the Israelites investigate "how these nations served their gods," their going a-whoring loses its metaphorical quality altogether and becomes plain whoring. We know from Herodotus and other classical writers that temple prostitution was universal in the Near East, both part time and full time. Nor can there be any doubt that the economic side of ritual prostitution played a great part in the shifting of preponderance from female to male priesthood and religion. Prenuptial prostitution was customary in many countries, and it was highly honorable for a girl to earn her dowry by prostitution. But as a married woman she was obliged to be faithful.

After two thousand years of Christianity, it is difficult for us to understand the institution of temple prostitution. It might become easier if we realize that both the sacred prostitute and the nun dedicate their sex to their gods. From time immemorial, it has been the universal belief that sexual behavior influences the course of events, such as success in hunting and abundance of crops. But whether it was indulgence or abstinence that brought success was a matter of regional conventions. And so the sacred prostitute dedicated her sex life to the benefit of life in this world and the honor of her god, as the nun denies hers and abstains to the glory of her God and the Other World.

The great temples of the ancient Near East were not merely temples but conglomerations like the Vatican City, only more complex. The confines enclosed temples, schools, libraries, archives, treasure houses, storehouses, whorehouses, a bank, stables, slaughterhouses, buildings for administration, and living quarters for the masses of people employed in the holy business.

It was his marriage that brought heartache and grief to Hosea. Bowed under "the burden of a prophet," he also suffered from the faithlessness of his wife, whom he had taken at Yahweh's request, and he could not help seeing some analogy between his sorrows and his God's. In complete disregard of Mosaic law and her conjugal duties, his wife does not care more for him than Israel and Judah do for Yahweh. And from now on in prophetic language the covenant becomes wedlock.

A monotheistic God is necessarily solitary, a state of affairs that "is not good" in God's own words. In a stroke of sheer genius Hosea joins Yahweh to his chosen people, thus making possible the legitimate use of the sacred-marriage imagery understood by everyone in the ancient Near East and dear to everyone's religious emotions and cravings: "I will betroth thee unto me forever; yea, I will betroth thee unto me in righteousness, and in judgment, and in lovingkindness, and in mercies. I will even betroth thee unto me in faithfulness: and thou shalt know the Lord" (Hosea 2:19).

By Yahweh's betrothal to his people, that is, to a body politic, the insoluble problem of sacred marriage in Monotheism is solved. This way Monotheism remains intact, and the primeval sacred marriage transcends its orgiastic origin and retains metaphysical meaning and sanctity. In the first four chapters of his book, Hosea has laid down the archetype of all biblical marriage imagery, and it may well be that his genius saved Yahwism in the thick of Near Eastern fertility religions. (Even fourteen hundred years later Mohammed had to face a similar predicament, and admitted, for similar reasons, a slight feminine touch into his teachings, to the despair of his commentators [surah 53:19].)

After Hosea's achievement in expressing the desired intimacy between God and his people in terms of matrimony, the picture changes, and God, the totalitarian creator-dictator, turns husband—a husband who serves longer and harder for his spouse than Jacob did, than any man ever did, for he "is God and not a man." This is not a love affair; this is wedlock. And what we witness now in the Old Testament is the first centuries of a unique marriage, or rather the tireless efforts to make this union work.

In the Western hemisphere it has become a prevailing notion that marriage, a serious social enterprise, should be a love match; should be based upon a state of severe intoxication called "being in love." Beyond the ensuing hangover in many cases no further endeavor is undertaken to achieve the desired unity, and the enterprise, launched with passionate fireworks, ends quickly in ashes. Eastern marriages, on the other hand, are prearranged, and sometimes the bridal couple meet at the wedding for the first time. In these matches love and loyalty are the goal to be reached by combined efforts in the course of marriage.

In the Prophets' conjugal vernacular, the ceaseless attempts to cope with this situation at times rather resemble the taming of the shrew. But the betrothed, be she Israel, Judah, Samaria, Zion, or Jerusalem, continues to be caught in flagrant adultery with Baalim, far from being aware of the new alliance and allegiance: "For the spirit of whoredom is in the midst of thee, and they have not known the Lord."

How could they? As if afraid of his own courage, Hosea employs the marriage imagery only at the beginning of his book. The Isaiahs use it only twice (54:5, 57). Jeremiah is less hesitant. But it is not until Ezekiel, at the time of the captivity, that the marriage terminology is used at its fullest and most explicit (16,23).

Here I must interrupt myself again: Ezekiel, Son of Man, is also an archaeological marvel. He was exiled

"among the captives by the river Chebar," which is Jubar,
a tributary of the Euphrates, the region of Tell Halaf and Brak
where the "Eye-Goddess" had her temples. And she
and all the inlaid eyes from Tell Halaf certainly left an imprint
on his visions. The "Scorpion-Man" gave him the creeps,
as many things from Tell Halaf can do to one. His verbal
portraitures of Assyrian wall paintings are excellent,
and so far as I know Ezekiel was the only one, except for
Layard, to describe these paintings before André Parrot
made them accessible to the public in 1961 in
his magnificent book, *The Arts of Assyria.*

In Ezekiel's words, Samaria "doted on her lovers, on the
Assyrians her neighbors, which were clothed with blue, captains
and rulers, all of them desirable young men, horsemen riding
upon horses . . . clothed most gorgeously. . . . She increased
her whoredoms: for when she saw men portrayed upon the wall,
the images of the Chaldeans portrayed with vermilion, girded
with girdles upon their loins, exceeding in dyed attire upon
their heads, all of them princes to look to, after the manner of
the Babylonians of Chaldea, the land of their nativity: and as
soon as she saw them with her eyes, she doted upon them, and
sent messengers unto them into Chaldea. And the Babylonians
came to her into the bed of love . . ." (23:5–6, 12–17).
This Prophet does not sit down by the waters of Babylon to
weep. After he has done his share of professional cursing, he sits
down to plan a new Jerusalem in detail and to revise the law.
Jeremiah poses and answers a crucial question at the beginning of his third chapter: "They say, If a man put away his
wife, and she go from him, and become another man's, shall he
return unto her again? shall not that land be greatly polluted?
but thou hast played the harlot with many lovers; *yet return
again to me,* saith the Lord." This is against his own law (Deut.
24:4). But he, after all, is the Lord, who can and does change his
mind more than once during the Old Testament. Deuteronomic
law differs from Mosaic law, and Jeremiah 3:1 differs from
Deuteronomy. And so the Lord said unto Jeremiah: "The backsliding Israel hath justified herself more than treacherous Judah.

Go and proclaim these words towards the north, and say, Return, thou backsliding Israel, saith the Lord; and I will not cause mine anger to fall upon you: for I am merciful, saith the Lord. . . . Turn, O backsliding children, saith the Lord; for I am married unto you."

Alternating between wrath and forgiveness, he goes on and on and on, as husbands do. Hosea, Jeremiah, and Ezekiel bear witness that marital brawls have continued unchanged for the last three thousand years. It is the perennial brawl, the standard brawl. The rage of the betrayed husband, the range and pattern of his reproaches and accusations, are the same today.

She did not have a penny, she was in rags when he picked her up. She is unworthy to be his wife. Small wonder, considering her background. Just look at her family: "As is the mother, so is the daughter. Thou art thy mother's daughter, that loatheth her husband and her children; and thou art the sister of thy sisters, which loathed their husbands and their children: your mother was an Hittite, and your father an Amorite" (Ezek. 16:44–5). "In the fire of his jealousy" he threatens to revenge himself, to do to her what she has done to him: "They have moved me to jealousy with that which is not God; . . . and I will move them to jealousy with those which are not a people; I will provoke them to anger with a foolish nation" (Deut. 32:21).

This is not matrimonial bliss. To make a go of this marriage is a hard and at times heartbreaking labor; and the Prophets are in despair, for they are the matchmakers. Hosea sums up the difficult situation very clearly: "For she said, I will go after my lovers, that give me my bread and my water, my wool and my flax, mine oil and my drink. . . . For she did not know that I gave her corn, and wine, and oil, and multiplied her silver and gold, which they prepared for Baal" (2:5). The situation is, admittedly, maddening. He, Yahweh, is the maker and giver of all her riches, but Israel, not knowing it, thankfully embraces the Baalim. "My people are destroyed for lack of knowledge. . . . My people ask counsel at their stocks, and their staff declareth unto them: for the spirit of whoredoms hath caused them to err, and they have gone a-whoring from under their God. They sacrifice upon the tops of the mountains, and burn incense upon the hills, under oaks and poplars and elms, because the shadow thereof is good: therefore your daughters shall commit whoredom, and your spouses shall commit adultery. Shall I not punish your daughters when they commit whoredom, or your spouses when they commit adultery? for themselves are separated with whores, and they sacrifice with harlots: therefore the people that doth not understand shall fall" (4:6, 12–14).

This is the theme repeated over and over again with variations in the prophetic polyphony of the Old Testament. It is the Prophets' ceaseless endeavor to make the people understand what they are talking about: the endeavor of the self-appointed missionary who feels called to impose his ideology upon people who are quite happy without him.

What the Prophets feel and indicate in their troubled eloquence is God's deep need for Man and for love. This God is not today's Ultimate Reality of the Universe. There was no such Universe at the time of Yahweh, who is solely concerned with his living image on earth, Man, the masterpiece with which he has topped his creation, and he expects his living image on earth to behave accordingly.

And that this is exactly what Man is doing becomes more and more evident. With all his shortcomings, he is the image of Yahweh, who is the only living God there ever was, the only God who can love and hate as one loves and hates oneself. How far he is from Unconditional Love, which is a Platonic idea and belongs to the Other World. It is his moral ambiguity and his absurdity that make him the living God. How one can feel and share his passion, his self-righteousness, his partiality, his irrational likes and dislikes! "Was not Esau Jacob's brother? saith the Lord: yet I loved Jacob, and I hated Esau" (Malachi 1:2–3). And in the next chapter he rages, "Why do we deal treacherously every man against his brother?" I adore him. *Viva Dios!*

Apropos Eighteen

I ALSO ADORE the way he has with successful kings. He cannot bring himself to punish them, but instead punishes their unsuccessful sons and grandsons. He couldn't do otherwise: for who can resist David, Solomon, and Ahab?

To read the "Lives" of Saul and David and their sons, all of them so tragically interwoven, is to read a group of the greatest "Lives" ever written. Samuel, the dark power behind them, won't yield an inch of his power to Saul without making him pay. He changes kings in midstream and anoints David. And since he cannot touch Saul, whom he has anointed first, he drives him out of his mind. In the immensely dark and powerful books of Samuel we see David rise against a cataract of blood.

But who can resist David? Indefatigably destroying the indestructible Amalekites and Philistines, he becomes Yahweh's dearest. David is not only the great conqueror and military reformer, he takes delight in music, instruments, and poetry. He serves the Lord with joy and singing. He dances before the Lord, and enriches the austere Yahweh-worship in a way that makes Amos' and other Prophets' hair stand on end. He takes Jerusalem by purchase and conquest, and Carmel he takes by marriage. He amasses fabulous riches, and also has the right son to spend them.

There is no war in Solomon's reign, and there is no end of

spending his father's riches. And in the beginning of his reign, "Judah and Israel were many, as the sand which is by the sea in multitude, eating and drinking, and making merry" (I Kings 4:20). And for once there is no sour note in eating and drinking and making merry. It might have marred the building activities. As for those buildings, they must have been an indescribable Phoenician technicolor splendor.

But who can resist Solomon, who loved gold and women so much, who wrote the Song of Songs, and of the four things too wonderful to behold: "The way of an eagle in the air; the way of a serpent on the rock; the way of a ship in the midst of the sea, and the way of a man with a maid" (Proverbs 30:19). There is a Solomonic touch in Mohammed when he says: "I have loved three things much: prayer, perfumes and women." And when Solomon is asked by Yahweh what he wants as a favor and he replies: "Give thy servant an understanding heart," it is almost more than one can bear without bursting into tears of joy. At his death, however, his country and people are exhausted, the monarchy is falling to pieces, and Judah and Israel are divided.

No other king after Solomon is given so much space in the Books of Kings as Ahab, and not only as a background for Elijah's performances. Of all kings Ahab, "who did more to provoke the Lord of Israel to anger than all the kings of Israel before him," who built ivory houses and ivory beds for his queen Jezebel, and was great in sin and war! But Yahweh lets him win a tremendous victory against the Syrians: a hundred thousand foot-men slain in one day, while twenty-seven thousand are crushed by a falling wall. What a wall! And when Ahab "went softly," Yahweh cannot resist: "I will not bring the evil in his days: but in his son's days will I bring the evil upon his house" (I Kings 21:29). Ahab's death is as splendid a death as that of El Cid: mortally wounded, he is "stayed up in his chariot against the Syrians" (22:35), and so he dies. But of his seventy-two sons not one fared well, and seventy were beheaded in one sentence.

Apropos Nineteen

AFTER incessant theological whitewashings, Yahweh vanishes gradually behind a blinding white glare. Who on
earth wants this heavenly Snow White? We would have
been left with a plaster God, had not the Old Testament been
preserved, where we can still find the living God as the old
ruffian in his full vigor. Although the edition of the Old Testament as we have it is not older than the fourth century B.C.,
and the compilers have already done a lot of whitewashing, parts
of it are still fresh and wonderfully free from plaster. With
the compilers, Satan comes in, and with the admittance of
Satan, Monotheism becomes but a name, a trade name covering
a host of intruders who came in during the last centuries B.C.
and after.

In the fourth century, the first Chronicle says (21:1): "And
Satan stood up against Israel, and provoked David to number
Israel." What Satan has replaced here is the unvarnished "anger
of the Lord" to be found earlier in the books of Samuel, who
used it so well. "And the anger of the Lord was kindled against
Israel, and he moved David against them to say, Go, number
Israel and Judah" (I Sam. 24:1). This shows Satan as God's own
bad temper, and a hell of a bad temper he can have. And thus
Monotheism is restored to me, and happily I leave all the white-
and eyewash to all who are happy with it.

Instead of snorting defiantly at the *lex talionis,* an eye for
an eye and a tooth for a tooth, we should rather
see it in its historical context and realize what a moral
achievement it actually was, as over the primitive institution
of blood feud and collective vengeance. In the earlier,
savage state of society, the next of kin had the "right" to wipe
out the culprit's family, clan or village, as the Nazis
did in Lidice and as we in our great magnanimity are setting
out to do with the Bomb. From this kind of savagery
the *lex talionis* is already a great moral step forward: it means,
do not do more harm than has been done to you,
do not take a head for a tooth. From there it is not far to
Confucius, who seems to have been the first to
express an idea that was already in the air, discernible in
Persian, Indian, Jewish, and Greek ideologies during the last
centuries B.C.: "Do not unto others as you do not want to be
done unto yourself." Aware of changing social conditions
around him, Yahweh changes his attitude and laws in the
course of the Old Testament. And "love thy neighbour as
thyself" is already recommended in Leviticus.
But the ten commandments are obviously still too
high a code of morals for us.

¶In the course of the Old Testament, God comes to know that
life on earth is an experience of unexpected complexity leading
to perpetual struggle, and he learns from these experiences. He
leaves Bronze Age feudalism and his utopia of an elite to the
Bronze Age, and widens his outlook to new horizons and his
heart to other nations. Willing to break down the wall of
Apartheid he erected round the dreams of his youth, he prepares
to join the commonwealth of nations.

And then comes Ezra, who has learned nothing and has to
start all over again: he re-erects the wall of Apartheid that has
brought so much wailing to the Jews. And this, as if Yahweh
had not explicitly abandoned his narrow tribalism and opened
his arms to all who keep his commandments. Whether Gentile,
son of stranger, or eunuch, "Even them will I bring to my holy

mountain, and make them joyful in my house of prayer . . . for my house shall be a house of prayer for all people" (Isa. 56:7) .

That it was a long, a lonely, and a hard way for Yahweh, as it is for his human images, to achieve mature tolerance and to accept failure, God's whitewashers would never admit, and he lets them have their own way. The dignity of his office as the Most High demands protocol, and what the Prophets give us are in effect "official bulletins" and no more. Stern and humorless in office, he displays a saving grace of humor in talmudic legends, where after a nine-hour day's work he settles down to play with Leviathan, "for Leviathan he had created for himself to play with."

He is not playful in the Bible, and after Noah's catastrophic hangover that caused more devastation than the Flood, there is a regrettable but understandable teetotaling vein in the Old Testament. Yahweh is a sober God, and the biblical flood-myth, dictated by morality, has lost the exuberant innocence of the original Sumerian flood-myth, where the gods, habitually in their cups, have got themselves in a sorry mess which they not only admit but loudly bewail.

> In contrast with other myths, it seems there was no Paradise
> Lost in Sumer, no Golden Age to lament for. Just the opposite
> took place: in the beginning there had been only gods, so
> that the gods had to do all the work themselves. This was
> reason enough to create human beings, who became "tenants"
> of the land, which of course remained the property
> of the gods, for whom they had to work it.
> And the gods never had it so good.

> While busily and boozily modeling human beings from clay,
> these gods, whose work made them thirsty, at length got tight
> and started to make all kinds of freaks, challenging one
> another to find a place in society for this one and that one.
> Thus the crooked and lame and all the misfits came into
> existence. The human beings, however, made in the image of

their gods, could also get thirsty and tight and at times
uproariously noisy, just when the gods wanted to sleep.
On one such occasion the gods lost their tempers and in a
collective tantrum drowned mankind in an eight-day flood—
only to find out to their perplexity that their own
existence depended entirely on their creatures' sacrifices
and services. There were no more sacrifices, for the
flood which the gods had so thoughtlessly sent had
turned their useful creatures into clay
again. Apparently no longer used and able to fend for
themselves, the starving gods in their despair started accusing
one another of having caused this catastrophe.
When finally they learned that Utnapishtim and his family had
survived in the ark, well able to repeople the earth,
they were overwhelmed with joy and gave him
and his wife immortality.

To the puritan Old Testament such a story is unacceptable,
not only because it is humorous, undignified, and immoral, but
because it reveals to a dangerous degree a state of affairs that
ought to be kept from human awareness forever: God's depen-
dence upon Man. Moses and the Prophets are determined to re-
verse this order, and after a titanic struggle they succeed; the
doctrine is taken up by Christianity and Islam and carried over
one half of the globe. From now on it is Man who depends
entirely on God, who gives up working and sits enthroned in
glorious inactivity.

In the two religions crystallizing in the Levant towards the
end of the Bronze Age, Yahwism and Orphism, a misanthropic
trait is too evident to be overlooked. The Eden and Prometheus
myths could not be more explicit: Man has against God's will
acquired knowledge and so raised himself "above the level of
beasts." Bronze Age clergy evidently considered this an en-
croachment on divine prerogatives, divine private property. To
prevent any recurrences and to discourage Man's appetite for
more apples from the tree of knowledge, sin was brandished as a

flaming sword, and proved a most effective deterrent. The Greeks accomplished the same with Hesiod's and Aeschylus' Prometheus myth. Zeus is not only indifferent towards Man, but becomes hostile when Prometheus, who deeply cares for mankind, teaches them to "harness" fire for firing bricks and pottery and for other arts and crafts that ease Man's lot and raise him "above the level of beasts." This was HYBRIS, and was punished cruelly. Knowledge was divine property, guarded and dispensed by the clergy, and pious ignorance has remained a virtue to the multitude until recently.

According to theology, God wants praise. Well, who doesn't? God and his images want praise and need it and should have it. But the old method of distribution, all praise to God and all blame on Man, does not work any longer, to the distress of theologians.

Yahweh gets all the praise Bronze Age gods and kings demanded and got. Moses and the Prophets make him lead the chorus of his own praises in the manner of Bronze Age sovereigns. Rameses II is a good case in point. The temples of Abu Simbel, built to restore the self-confidence of Egypt that was badly shaken after the Hyksos, contain a prototype of this grandiloquence, which served a religio-political purpose at a time when religion and politics were the same thing. Rameses as God-Pharaoh of Egypt addresses himself to the world and posterity in what looks like the most vainglorious self-praise, meant to restore the prestige of the national god incarnate. Since the end sanctifies the means, the battle against the Hittites at Kadesh, a rather close shave, is described by Rameses as an overwhelming and tremendous victory, regardless of the facts recorded by his own scribes in less spectacular places. His dynastic marriage to a Hittite princess, documented on the famous "Marriage Stele," did not hinder him from referring to her father as "this miserable Hittite." But the marriage was a success.

After centuries of thundering self-demonstrations, Yahweh's marriage also becomes a success. And when he throws "your father was a Hittite" into Jerusalem's face in a jealous rage, it is meant more as an insult than as a historical statement.

When he becomes "husband," he is shown as a stern, self-righteous, domineering husband, quick-tempered but of boundless endurance. He never admits failures, but never hesitates nor tires in demonstrating his jealousy. He is the jealous God par excellence.

Last Apropos

I F THE DURABILITY of a marriage is a criterion, and it can be, Yahweh's marriage to his people must be called an unsurpassed success. After a tumultuous and at times utterly discouraging first millennium, a vast, deep and reciprocal involvement is reached that has lasted to the present day. The outlook at first seemed hopeless, and it has taken a truly godly perseverance on his part to make her see the point and to win her cooperation. And this God, whose image we are, shows us that this goal cannot be reached by spectacular tricks alone, but by honest toil and sweat and tears, by incessant struggle and effort. His dilemma is ours, and in his wrath and suffering he is close to the human heart.

¶He promised too much in the beginning, as is the way of husbands—and wives. He promised security in an insecure world. And when things go wrong, he reacts in a way well known to all of us: first he puts the blame on her (and she is, by God, not blameless), and then he doubles his promises: "For brass I will bring gold, and for iron I will bring silver. . . . I will lay thy foundations with sapphires. And I will make thy windows of agates, and thy gates of carbuncles." Sweet and foolish things, meant to soothe. And finally—both worn out and weary and both in need of comfort—his moving "let's forget and start afresh": "Behold, I create new heavens and a new earth:

and the former shall not be remembered" (Is. 60:17, 54:11-12, 65:17).

Doesn't this have a familiar ring to married ears? Most of the Prophets were married men, and they knew. And in the end, behold, this becomes one of those marriages where one knows for certain that he will never survive her death; and the first marriage counsel, given to Adam, to cleave to his wife, does not remain an empty phrase, for nobody else clave as Yahweh did.

And now this God, "acquainted with grief," is no longer a vague apparition: he is Megalo-Anthropos, MAN writ large, as, correctly reasoned, he is bound to be if Man is his image. Like his images he cannot live without love. And as Megalo-Anthropos, with all the inconsistencies and ambivalence of his images, he shows us as no other god how to endure come hell or high water.

> Far too primitive for "abstract reasoning," I have failed to
> come to any *modus vivendi* with the Ultimate Reality,
> but end as I began, with an image of God that is necessarily
> anthropomorphic. What I heard as a child about God struck
> me as uncannily "familiar" in terms of my
> thundering father, whom I suspected to be omniscient and
> who frightened me. And when I now, towards the end
> of my life and in pursuit of the Pillars of Hercules, withdrew
> into my own wilderness to read the Old Testament,
> I encountered in it the autobiography of God, whose images
> we are. And in the pathos of Yahweh
> and his immense loneliness, never mentioned to me by
> theologians, I found again an only too familiar human
> situation: our loneliness, our quest for love, and the endless
> and painful process of maturing and enduring.

And it is the overwhelming proximity of God's pathos as Megalo-Anthropos that gives at last a true and beautiful meaning to the hitherto meaningless phrase that Man is God's image.

"How can it harm me if I understand the writer's meaning in a different sense from that in which another understands it?" asked Augustine in his *Confessions* (12.18). How indeed?

Humanists and Marxists alike want to abolish God from their world. They are free to do so. "God is unnecessary," they say. So is beauty, so is art, one could reply. Free to choose, I would say let us have all three of them. And science and plumbing too. Not to forget humanism. Let us not miss any of the good things. What did Saint Thérèse of Lisieux say, when pressed to make up her mind? "I choose everything."

Thus I think we would grievously deprive ourselves if we excluded God from our minds. God, this tremendous, this deep and fascinating dream of boundless interpretability! Why blame the dream, when ecclesiastical interpreters turned it into a nightmare? And why, furthermore, this bitter resentment for having dreamed and believed in this dream?

Like an adolescent who will forgive neither his father nor himself for having believed in Santa Claus, I found it hard to overcome a rather silly resentment against God and my former belief. Aware that I had outgrown the faculty of belief as I had outgrown the faculty of childbearing, I had come to the conclusion that believing is comparable to the function of the thymus gland: enormous in infancy, it normally vanishes with advancing years. But the resentment remained—until at last I remembered Old Dessauer: one ought to respect the dreams of one's youth. The resentment evaporated and my outlook changed: there was the promised new heaven, and a fresh and refreshing vista opened upon the young God who weathered so many storms and underwent the metamorphosis from the revengeful Lord of Hosts to the God "who has put the strong love of life between Man and his despair" (Firenzuola).

"The Church's concern will be less and less an obsession with exactly what God tells the Pope," said the English Archbishop

Roberts in 1965 in Rome. "Now we are interested in exactly *what kind of person God is.*" The Old Testament reveals God as the archetype and very image of the complete person. Not the perfect, but the complete human being; for without the element of evil Man is incomplete, is a freak. God as Yahweh is whole, is the sum total of human possibilities, from the best to the worst, from the sublime to the absurd. He has been our lodestar, he has been with us from the beginning of time, and our past was brutish and long. He tried to impose order upon his integral chaos and to overcome evil, and after many relapses into brutishness he succeeded. Again and again his high hopes were dashed, and he erupted in savage and cataclysmic rages. He also fathomed the abyss of loneliness and grief; but he never gave in and never gave up, and thus set us an example of tenacity and resilience, always ahead of himself and determined to change the world.

Of all the gods of antiquity he was the only one to become holy. The nimbus has surrounded him from Isaiah to the present day, from the emergence of metaphysics to its end. Mental climates change, and we have witnessed in our time a drastic change: twenty-five hundred years of metaphysical speculations have come to an end and in a drier mental climate the nimbus is no longer visible, but God appears as archetypal Man instead.

How can one recognize him but with a happy smile, the peculiar and universal expression of recognition, the herald of laughter? Had not laughter been the response he met before the dawn of metaphysics in Abraham and Sarah? "God has brought me laughter," she said.

He is as equivocal as gods have always been and as his images are. Before "the failure of nerve" the gods of the Greeks were utterly ambiguous and often rather un-divine. They were neither good nor bad, they were both, and they were close to the human heart. Then Apollo was upgraded to a lifeless and bloodless paragon of reason stripped to the bone, an epitome of self-restraint and clarity, of nobility and beauty, of purity and perfection. This impeccable bore and plaster god, the ideal of the good and the beautiful, had been called by the ancient Greeks "the crooked one," and crooked he was indeed, apart from many other things. As "the far-shooter," he was vindictive, relentless and cruel and made Achilles rage: "You worst of all the Gods!"; and in Euripides' *Ion* he raped, he lied and hedged and was a perfect cad. He was alive then, and not yet turned into plaster. And Zeus had used unfair means to overcome his unfair father; he also had his marital troubles, and he lorded it over the other gods in Bronze Age fashion for several centuries, laughing at the predicament of men. But after Homer and Hesiod he had had his day, and he never again gets a clear shape. Classical Greece—which means Athens, obsessed with democracy and philosophy—had no use for a king, and the retired Zeus ends as one of the twelve Olympians in democratic fashion.

Not so Yahweh! He wanted to lord it over all the other gods, and he did in the end, for more than two millennia, surviving kingdoms and constitutions. But unfortunately New Testament theologians did everything they could to dehumanize this God, robbed him of all his inconsistencies, imperfections, and absurdities; they rarefied his substance until he went up like a divine gas, no longer perceptible.

Philosophy replaced him with the Ultimate Reality, an opaque abstraction that eclipsed the living God—and dread and anguish settled upon a world we had at last rendered godless. To Existentialists he became the Other or dead or both, and they feel abandoned. As the Other he is alien, they say. Doesn't that depend on the language the linguistic game is played in? In English and German the Other is and remains an alien and different from us. But not in French and Spanish, where the Other can be both: he can be an alien and he can be an ally, one of *nous-autres, nos otros*. Our metaphysical goggles prevented us from seeing this. But in spite of having discarded these goggles and looking Existence straight in the eye, Existentialists pride themselves on being abandoned.

As to the statement "God is dead"—do gods die? The dying

gods had their perennial deaths and resurrections and will do so to the end of time. Other gods of antiquity moved silently, in the disguise of saints or devils, into the bosom of the Church; and in poetry and art they continue to live and have their being undiminished and undisguised to the present day, which shows that the existence of gods does not depend necessarily on worship and belief.

Today's rumor that God is dead has an unmistakable gnostic flavor. Two thousand years ago in a mental climate similar to ours, a time of *Götterdämmerung,* the Gnostics diagnosed God as bad. They tried to depreciate him and to deny him his legitimate position. The Existentialists, radically diagnosing him as dead, remind me of a funeral congregation before the reading of the will. Skeptical about his alleged riches, they tend to be almost convinced that the deceased has long been bankrupt. They feel bereft, and gloomily expect to be deprived of a legacy they once foolishly expected.

But in the Old Testament, Yahweh openly made his will, investing his substance first in the Jews and later in "the nations." This immense substance of boundless stamina, teeming creativity and unbroken pride and confidence, has given the Jewish nation their unique qualification for endurance, survival, and revival in the face of never-ending onslaughts on their race, the last one the slaughter of six million Jews in the heart of Europe, a memorial to the Nordic race and her glory.

Seen with secular eyes and not in a glass darkly, Yahweh has grown from what Marx called "the imaginary substance of the tribe" to the authentic substance of Man, and the Old Testament is his autobiography and anthropology in one.

Viva Dios! His indubitable humanity, his cognate nature with Man that is so obvious in the Old Testament, has been concealed by theologians who, through their metaphysical training, had lost the faculty of using the secular eye. They upheld the myth of a perfect God, who created not only this sinful world but also two millennia of bad conscience.

This myth of the remote and perfect God has alienated Him from Us. Aristotle seemed aware of it when he wrote in his *Ethics* that "removed to a great distance, as God is, the possibility of friendship ceases" (III.7). And yet it did not hinder him from driving the wedge deeper. This wedge has to go now, for it has separated us for so long from "the Friend behind phenomena."

The Pillars of Hercules II

WHERE ARE the Pillars of Hercules? It looks as if, tossed on the sea of my unruly thoughts, I had lost sight of them. To be honest, I had. Until the Abbé Pluche came to my rescue. His book *"Histoire du Ciel*, Quatrieme Edition, revûë et corrigée par Ms. L'Abbé Pluche [the name added by hand], La Haye, 1744," had been right in front of me all those months, but remained unopened, for its size and the color of its binding made it an ideal base for a beautiful Spanish head of John the Baptist. When finally I decided to give the head a wooden base, I opened the book and found the Abbé etymologizing in all the dead languages including the Semitic. Etymology is a most engaging and slightly paranoid language game of old, vigorously played by mythologists from Plato on, but not always rewarding. Today's mythologists agree on the barbarian origin of the Greek gods' names. But when it comes to etymology, most of them, instead of looking for barbarian, *i.e.*, non-Greek, roots for these names, turn with one accord to the Greek root-field and, flexing their classical biceps, keep on pulling Greek roots which, if one can swallow them at all, leave one listless and undernourished.

Not so the Abbé Pluche. Living in a world still uncomplicated by Indo-European problems, and aided by his ardor to harmonize ancient myths with the Bible, he comes up with a cornucopia of Semitic roots, delightful and wholesome, a joy to my palate and a blessing to this book. For in my quest for the legitimate Hercules, propelled by wrath about Graecomania and anti-Semitism, at the very last moment Pluche, the Abbé *ex machina,* comes to my assistance in a way that surpasses my wildest dreams.

Hercules, he writes on page 256, comes from Egypt, and was passed on to the Greeks and others by the Phoenicians. A Hercules was a representative of Horus, the young god as warrior, a member of the small elect groups of distinguished young warriors, *gendarmes,* defending precincts against wild beasts, robbers, and brigands. These young heroes were called Heracli or Herculi or Horecli, a name derived from the Semitic *horim,* "illustrious young men" (Eccl. 10:17, Nehem. 6:17) and *keli,* "armed." The Phoenicians, says Pluche, gave their Horecli the epithet Ben Alcum or Ben Alcmen, "the invincible son," which in the end became Heracles the son of Alcmena. And it looks as if myth-making was not entirely *ein Urvorgang* shrouded in metaphysical fog, but at times clear pun and fun.

Wherever the Phoenicians founded their trading stations and erected their sacred pillars, a group of Sidonian or Tyrian Herculi went to guard them, the most famous being those of Cadiz. These far-flung Herculi, says Pluche on page 267, had been obliged, it seems, to undergo instruction in astronomy and Atlantic geography. This did not go down at all well with the young muscle-heads, who evidently mistook the priesthood's astronomical instruction as an attempt to unburden themselves. Although this might sound highly sarcastic and conjectural, Greek myth shows that it was the way Alcmena's son looked at the matter.

When the Egyptian elite corps coagulates in Greek myth into one single hero, his myth gets puzzling at times. How the Abbé Pluche's revelations would have relieved Pausanias, who cannot get over the tall tale that Heracles started his heroic career in Thespiae, chasing lions by day and sleeping with the king's fifty daughters by night (9.27.6)! This cannot be "his" Heracles, he decides, not the son of Alcmena; this sounds more like the one "of whom I found sanctuaries at Erythrae in Ionia and at

Tyre." He continues, "The sanctuary of Mycalesian Demeter is entrusted to the Idean Heracles," and he wonders about all the various sanctuaries "entrusted" to Heracles or "closed every night and opened again by Heracles." They had been entrusted to the groups of young heracli, armed with clubs, who later in Greece got sanctuaries of their own as Heracles Alexikakos, Defender from Evil.

Herodotus describes the club-men engaged in mock combat at the Horus festival at Papremis (2.63–4). "A sharp fight with clubs ensued" between the horecli of Horus and the horecli of Isis. And speaking about the special privileges of the Egyptian warrior class and elite guards Herodotus says that the Pharaoh's bodyguard gets, besides tax-free land, five pounds of bread, two pounds of beef, and four cups of wine daily (2.168). I always wondered why the Greeks liked to depict their young Heracles with a horn of plenty. And also why the handsome Kouros loses his looks and grows into the beefy and starchy frame of the full-blown Greek hero. Now I know.

The Abbé is not altogether easy reading. With awesome, almost Gravesian sweeps, he gathers vast amorphous heaps of stunning facts and statements like those that baffle the Philistine readers of the great Balearic slinger. He also has harsh words for Virgil. But his Semitic roots are a true Sesame to antique common sense or nonsense.

Hunger makes food venerable, hunger deifies food, is more or less the Abbé's argument. Thus the Philistines worshiped Adirdagath, which the Greeks found unpronounceable and turned into Atergatis. Adirdagath stems from *adir,* "magnificent, great," and from *dag,* "fish." Consequently Dagon should be the male fish-god, the merman of the Philistines, whose image was overthrown and mutilated in the first book of Samuel when the captured Ark of God was placed next to him. "Only the stump (or fishy part) of Dagon was left to him" (5:4).

Next Aphrodite arises from the Abbé's cornucopia. The Cypriote Phoenicians called her Appherudoth, from *pherudoth,* "seed," as in Joel 1:17. She is all seeds, crops, fertility. The

Greek tongue made Aphrodite of her, a phonetic rendering without sense, says Pluche, until they "recognized" the Greek element *aphros* "foam," in the name and whipped up their aetiological and frivolous Aphrodite myth.

According to Pluche, the whole Greek theogony is more or less the outcome of Semitic puns on the one side, and the Greeks' notorious refusal to learn foreign languages on the other. Resulting misunderstandings were deliberately fostered by fun-loving Phoenicians, says the Abbé, himself full of unconcealed mirth when it comes to analyzing the origin of pagan myths. He is a delightful "harmonizer" who has legitimate fun, jolly good learned fun, making game of the Greeks to the honor of God. The field of mythology, dreadfully befogged nowadays, he enters with the self-confidence of a crack shot, and most of his linguistic interpretations are a clean hit.

To epitomize the Abbé's extremely modern doctrine: the hardship of ancient days—to him the immediate post-diluvian days, those miserable muddy days that drove Noah to drink—drove people to worship their staple food, fish at the shores and grain inland. Regarding the grain, the Abbé adds a most precious footnote: there was Perephatta, from *peri*, "corn, crop, fruit," and from *patar*, "missing, lost." This would make Perephatta the Lost Crop. And Persephone, from *peri* and *saphan*, "hidden," the Hidden Crop, stored in bins. And this two hundred years before Cornford!

I was happy for days after this footnote, singing the glory that was Pluche. There is no other but Pluche! His comment on Moloch remains unsurpassed: "On bruloit en son honneur les enfans qu'on avoit de trop" (p. 179).

My French (Canadian) is no longer what it used to be, and without a dictionary within borrowing distance I must at times rely on myself, which is no more risky than relying on someone else in this myth business. But I think even with perfect seventeenth-century French I could only partly follow Pluche through his Dionysos. The Orphic Church had trouble enough working this deity, with his almost too savage past, into Olympus. The Abbé's etymological argument is again splendid. A Phoenician interpreter at an Egyptian or Cretan festival might have tried to make it clear: Dionysos is not the divine son but something similar; he claims to be the son, but is in fact *ben simeleh,* from *simeleh,* "simile, imitation." A true son, he would have explained, is one who comes out of his father's loins, or thigh in Semitic languages (Gen. 35:11, 46:26). And the Greeks took this *façon de parler* literally.

That hereabout lies the origin of the Semele myth I readily believe, though I cannot fully underwrite the Abbé's conclusions.

As is well known, the Phoenicians told tall tales like all sailors, and the Greeks fell for them. But when the Abbé doubts the Greeks' readiness to believe such rubbish, he overlooks the irresistibility of the absurd: it was this clumsy tale that "made" Dionysos and became the vehicle of Orphism. It was the great opportunity for the Orphics to promote their god, it was their *conceptio immaculata,* and raised their god to the rank of an Olympian. The unborn Dionysos is sewn into Zeus' thigh, and through this theological surgery he becomes the uniquely begotten son of the most high Olympian, the Mystery Child of the Orphics, who were always so bent on the marvelous and mysterious. Apollo, his greatest rival, was also son of Zeus, but borne by Leto. Whereas Dionysos was not borne by a woman, for Semele had vanished before the radiance of Zeus. He was begotten by Zeus and borne by Zeus, and there never had been such a son of Zeus. And thus the Thracian Dionysos, this immigrant from a barbarous country where, according to ancient authors, people had bouts of drunkenness in the woods and were fond of music, was accepted into Olympus, the most snobbish pantheon of the Levant.

Hercules, who never passed the rank of a popular patron saint, never really reached Olympus; but he reached the New World instead, where his pillars became the supreme symbol. Planted on Spanish soil at about the time of David and Solomon, the Pillars of Hercules became, and still are, the emblem of Spain. They acquired the meaning of the mottoes they were later to bear: *Ne Plus Ultra,* nothing more beyond. They marked a limit, a westward boundary, until conquering Spain proudly dropped the *Ne* and the pillars could bear the promise, *Plus Ultra.* And it proved no empty promise.

This promising continent, however, could not be held by Spain. Nor, for that matter, could it be held by Holland, France, or England. Under the sign of the pillars America started a life of her own, exceedingly *plus ultra,* to be derided by the resentful old European countries, who take their hardened arteries for monuments of culture, the only true culture there ever was, based on the Glory that was Greece.

America's population is an amalgam of other countries' malcontents, undesirables, cranks, adventurers, and also fugitives with brain power, vision, and integrity, who went there and still go there, where daydreams come true. But it was not the sign of the cross that made America victorious in the world, it was a sign much older than the cross: the Pillars of Hercules. They still stand for the "Good Life" Mesopotamia dreamed of, and for the way of life the Sidonians of Phoenicia led, in the words of the Prophets, "careless, quiet and secure." And who in his right mind would not wish for such a life, including the Americans, who have not yet fully reached this goal. But no other nation has ever to the same extent and scale endeavored and accomplished so much for the physical well-being of mankind in this world, so grievously neglected under the sign of the cross. Getting old I find nothing more comforting than comfort, which means to me two things only: good heating and good plumbing. Not to forget the *sine qua non:* books, thanks to the Phoenicians, for according to an Egyptian papyrus "behold, nothing surpasses books."

As I am not an American, I can with detachment enjoy watching the rest of the world sneering in loud derision at America and her way of life, and coveting and copying her as best it can. Copying her, asking for and receiving her aid, and remaining anti-American all the same, whether ally or foe. And the parallel to anti-Semitism is obvious. For thousands of years the world has borrowed ideologies of Semitic origin, and remained anti-Semitic all the time.

Looking back at our road towards humanity through the telescope of the Old Testament, history, and prehistory, I cannot share today's pessimism. History can be discouraging, but it offers also a spirited vista: the fact that Man has survived his own ideologies is encouraging indeed. It borders on the miraculous, and fills me with skeptical confidence in the future of Homo Sapiens despite himself. "Do not hanker after quick results," Confucius said.

References

Albright, W. F., *The Archaeology of Palestine*. Penguin Books, 1960.

Bertrand, Louis, and Charles Petrie, *The History of Spain*. Eyre and Spottiswoode, 1934.

Campbell, Joseph, *The Hero with a Thousand Faces*. Pantheon, 1949.

Cassirer, Ernst, *An Essay on Man*. Doubleday, 1953.

Childe, V. Gordon, *The Dawn of European Civilization*. Routledge and Kegan Paul, 1957. 6th ed.

Diodorus Siculus, *The Historical Library* (tr. G. Booth). London, 1814. 2 vols.

Frankfort, Henri, *Art and Architecture of the Ancient Orient*. Penguin Books, 1959.

Frankfort, Henri *et al.*, *Before Philosophy: the intellectual adventure of ancient man*. Penguin Books, 1949.

Frazer, Sir James G., *The Golden Bough: a study in comparative religion*. Macmillan, 1911–15. 12 vols.

Gibbon, Edward, *The History of the Decline and Fall of the Roman Empire*. Oxford University Press, 1903–06. 7 vols.

Gurney, O. R., *The Hittites*. Penguin Books, 1952.

Harrison, Jane E., *Ancient Art and Ritual*. Holt, 1913.

Herodotus, *History* (tr. George Rawlinson). Dent, 1910. 2 vols.

Hole, Edwin, *Andalus: Spain under the Muslims*. Dufour (Chester Springs, Pa.), 1958.

Hu-Shih, *The Development of the Logical Method in Ancient China*. Shanghai, 1922.

James, E. O., *Myth and Ritual in the Ancient Near East*. Barnes and Noble, 1961.

Josephus, *Works* (tr. St. J. Thackeray *et al.*). Heinemann, 1926–63. 8 vols. (Loeb Classical Library).

Jung, C. G., *Mysterium Coniunctionis*. Pantheon, 1963.

Murray, Gilbert, *Five Stages of Greek Religion*. Columbia University Press, 1925.

Parrot, André, *The Arts of Assyria*. Odyssey, 1962.

Polybius, *Histories* (tr. W. R. Paton). Heinemann, 1922–27. 6 vols. (Loeb Classical Library).

Procopius, *Histories of the Wars* (tr. by H. B. Dewing). Heinemann, 1914–40. 7 vols. (Loeb Classical Library).

Strabo, *Geography* (tr. H. C. Hamilton and W. Falconer). Bohn, 1848.

Toynbee, A. J., *A Study of History*. Oxford University Press, 1946. Abridged ed.

White, T. H., *The Book of Beasts: being a translation from a Latin bestiary of the twelfth century*. Putnam, 1954.

Zimmer, Heinrich, *Myths and Symbols in Indian Art and Civilization*. Pantheon, 1946.

About the Author

Greta Wels-Schon lives in Spain. This is her first book, the product of a long life, which has led her from Germany, to Canada, and finally to Spain. Before Hitler, she wrote for three or four German and Swiss magazines. She is seventy-one.